THE
ROTHMANS BOOK
OF
VILLAGE CRICKET

THE
ROTHMANS BOOK
OF
VILLAGE CRICKET

Patrick Murphy

Photographs by Paul Barker

BLOOMSBURY

First published in Great Britain 1992

Bloomsbury Publishing Limited, 2 Soho Square, London W1V 5DE

in association with Rothmans (UK) Limited

Text copyright © 1992 by Patrick Murphy

Chapter 4 copyright © 1992 by T.A.L. Huskinson

Photographs copyright © 1992 by Paul Barker

The moral right of the authors has been asserted

A CIP catalogue record for this book

is available from the British Library

ISBN 0 7475 1183 7

Edited and designed by Toucan Books Limited, London

Printed by HarperCollins Manufacturing, Glasgow

Contents

Acknowledgements

SO MANY PEOPLE have been very kind in helping me compile this project. It is a subject about which I feel very strongly. If village cricket declines terminally, part of this country's quality of life goes with it. The heart of many villages is being ripped out by the property developer, the estate agent and the compliant commuter who treats his new domicile as a dormitory and puts nothing into the community. People should live in a village to enjoy that particular locality's cricket, otherwise the club will wither away. The relentless creeping of motorway tentacles, the over-reliance on the car, the imperative of moving somewhere - anywhere - to find a job: all of that combines to dilute the roseate glow of cricket on the village green. Imperceptibly, life gets more pressurised as the millennium approaches and even more money has to be earned to satisfy our heightened material and social expectations that have been fed by the marketing men. A game of cricket in a sleepy village with the chime of the church clock the only interruption ought to be the natural antidote to all that modern hassle, but such days in the time warp need altruistic, voluntary work. Cricket clubs, and their thatched pavilions, comfortable dressing-rooms, sumptuous teas and lush outfields, do not just *happen*. Young players please note: your playing heritage is at stake here. A volunteer offers so much more than a surly, press-ganged teenager.

Whittling my list down from such a cornucopia of clubs has been an interesting exercise in self-delusion. Advice has been sought and willingly given by journalistic colleagues such as David Hopps, Chris Lander, Alan Lee, Graham Otway, John Helm, Christopher Martin-Jenkins, Ben Brocklehurst, Peter Hayter, Roger Protz and Nico Craven. The photographer, Paul Barker, has willingly disappeared into the hinterland of Britain, driving along narrow country lanes with a map balanced on his knees, and my imprecise instructions in his hand. Not once did he upbraid me for sending him on a few chases recognised by wild geese and I thank him for his forbearance and the excellence of his contribution. I am also indebted to Tony Huskinson for his comprehensive history of the Village Cricket Championship.

The reaction from officials of the selected clubs was highly gratifying. The pride in the ambience, playing performances and locations of their clubs permeated almost every sentence uttered and I have been deluged with faxes, brochures, club histories, fixture cards and telephone numbers for further information. The warmth and generosity Paul Barker and I have encountered simply confirmed my belief that cricket continues to be a very civilised sport, with many behavioural assets. I am grateful for the unstinting co-operation of dedicated club servants like Geoff Last at Outwood, Eric Gordon from Adlestrop, Oliver Comins at Warborough, Peter Chapman from Mobberley, Jeff Driver at Saltaire, Colin Young from Southborough, and so many more. My thanks to the club officials from all the featured grounds.

PATRICK MURPHY

Foreword

by
Graham Gooch

HAVING KNOWN Pat Murphy for many years now, I am delighted that he has published his views on how the village game should be played. Whenever we meet, he tells stories of recent exploits in villages up and down the country with his BBC Pebble Mill XI. As far as I can tell, Pat's definition of the perfect village match involves the absence of car noise, the church clock chiming and – above all – some quality real ale in the nearby pub. When our mutual friend, Bob Willis turned out for Pat's team at Sheepscombe, he was pleased to see how much excellent beer was consumed by the team before the match. Bob volunteered to open the batting after his second pint and was hit on the head off the first ball of the game; he vowed never to play village cricket again.

Having played Club Cricket as a youngster for Ilford, I know how much enthusiasm there is for the game at grassroots level. Pat is right to mention those players who love the game so much. They keep going for years, every summer weekend, even though the bowling arm gets lower and fielding just means sticking out a hand and hoping for the best. Good luck to them all, and the hard-working officials who keep the village clubs going. Those of us involved in the professional game appreciate how important cricket is to village life. Pat's book is a fine tribute to the players and officials on the village green.

Chapter 1

THE HISTORY OF VILLAGE CRICKET

'A rural cricket match in buttercup time, seen and heard through
the trees; it is surely the loveliest scene in England and the
most disarming sound. From the ranks of the unseen dead for ever
passing along our country lanes on their eternal journey, the
Englishmen fall out for a moment to look over the gate of the
cricket field and smile.'
Sir James Barrie

THE CREATOR OF Peter Pan was not known for his cynicism and realists who have played village cricket for a few years may well blanch at J. M. Barrie's roseate view, but it would take a grim soul to deny that the game on the village green has staved off the excesses of the modern world rather more successfully than the version played to a wider audience for the benefit of television, and the Hydra-headed monster that is money. Many a cricket-lover still draws comfort from watching the village game, rather than the increasingly anonymous, relentless fare served up in the Test arena. On the village green, there is character on offer, a relishable cocktail of the ambitious, the plodding and the realistic. The customs of the famous - courtesy of television's baleful influence - are aped by a few impressionable dreamers but humour and commonsense does keep breaking through and those who don helmet and visor or opt for histrionic pressurising of umpires are eventually marginalised.

There seems a tacit acceptance among village green cricketers that the revered customs and practices of the grand old game are still worth preserving. When your cricket skills are practically non-existent it does seem rather silly to make a fool of yourself with behaviour sadly commonplace now on the international circuit. The first straight ball or a dolly catch is usually enough to discomfit many fanatical village cricketers and long may the gap between illusions and realities be so wide.

The history of village cricket is basically a mirror of the changing social mores of this country. The village green has long been the very heart of a rural community. It was the area for grazing, for drawing of water and for handing out rough justice with the stocks to miscreants. There is an area in the village of Bearsted near Maidstone which encapsulates the role of the village green. It was the place where the great Alfred Mynn underlined his great cricketing

skills in the nineteenth century, five centuries earlier yet Wat Tyler and his supporters gathered there to prepare for their march on London during the Peasants' Revolt. The village green has reflected the changes in the social life of the people down through the ages, a fact recognised by the eminent historian G. M. Trevelyan. In his *English Social History* he saw village cricket in idyllic terms, writing of 'squire, farmer, blacksmith and labourer with their women and children come to see the fun, at ease together and happy all summer afternoon'.

Trevelyan believed that blissful state helped promote social stability and although the activities of Republicans, Chartists, Suffragettes and other dissenters have disturbed the status quo of the country the underlying desire for peaceful co-existence has been reflected in cricket's ability to soothe the savage breast - and beast. So squire and blacksmith could meet on equal terms on the village square and if both vicar and squire owed their places in the side to their social rather than cricketing standing in the community, that was simply a reflection of the old order of a less egalitarian age.

Today the yuppie with the carphone seems to have more time for the weekend games than the

farmer wrestling with the small print of the Common Agricultural Policy. And when did you last see a village blacksmith take in another reef of his belt, spit on his hands and roar in downhill off his long run? He has gone to the same economic oblivion as the village saddler, the tanner and the sexton. For centuries the yeoman stock of England would be born, reared and would die in the same place with little knowledge of a world outside their parish, apart from the time when the honour of their country had to be defended on a foreign field. Playing cricket for the village was as natural as

tugging the forelock to a nobleman and watching the vicar's flighted dross being carted into the meadow by opposition batsmen, when the labourer's lad would have nipped all that in its infancy with a few fast, straight deliveries. The Industrial Revolution and the motor car changed that, offering freedom of movement and greater self-reliance to the working man. Now it is common for the majority of players in the village side to travel a fair distance to the ground; many simply cannot afford to live in the villages they proudly represent on the cricket field.

The earliest reference to cricket is in Bede's *Life of St Cuthbert*, in the early part of the twelfth century. It evolved as the sport of shepherd boys on the downs of south-east England, where the sheep helped crop the grass and the ball was made up of matted sheep's wool. For several centuries, cricket was confined to that corner of England - particularly Kent - and by the start of the eighteenth century it was acquiring an economic significance. With licences now available for the sale of beer at matches, cricket was attracting large crowds. Money changed hands as wagers were struck and aristocratic patrons with private grounds saw the game as a diversion which could also yield a great deal of money. Sometimes matches were played for as much as a hundred guineas a side and sharp practice was not unknown. One day the Duke of Richmond's team was attacked by a mob for arriving late at a match in Surrey, in the process failing to give the opposition time enough to force a win. *Plus ça change* and all that; pragmatic captains like W.G. Grace and Ian Chappell would appear naïve choirboys in contrast to those early cricketing entrepreneurs with an eye for the main chance. Kerry Packer would have relished the infighting.

By the middle of the eighteenth century, several successful rural clubs had established some form of hegemony. The Duke of Richmond's team from the village of Slindon in West Sussex was good enough to beat Surrey by an innings; Dartford was the unofficial Kent team, playing all-England and Surrey on merit, while Sevenoaks (backed by the Duke of Dorset) chalked up many lucrative victories. Yet all the teams had to yield the palm to Hambledon. The windswept Broadhalfpenny Down near the Hampshire village of Hambledon is often erroneously referred to as 'The Cradle of Cricket', even though the game had been played in many other parts of south-east England before this club was formed. Hambledon CC's abiding value to

cricket is that it was the first to achieve lasting success and to have those achievements recorded in permanent form.

John Nyren, son of the former landlord of the Bat and Ball Inn (which still occupies a central position beside the ground) wrote two classic books about the club, including the deeds of his father, Richard - captain, groundsman and secretary during the club's halcyon period. Between 1772 and 1781 Hambledon CC beat all-England twenty-nine times; in 1772, they even beat Twenty Two of

England; in 1777 one of their matches marks the first recorded instance of three stumps being used and in the same year they beat all-England by an innings, the first time such a margin had been achieved. More than twenty thousand saw them play all-England in a game in 1772 and, thanks to John Nyren's writing, we have a clear account of the club's best players and its crucial role in the development of the game from village level to the Test arena. Hambledon's players were very professional, ahead of their time; they knew how to adapt to the hilltop grounds of Hampshire, with the ground sloping away sharply. They were proud men, wearing sky-blue coats with velvet collars, gold tricorn hats, white breeches and buckle shoes. In the field, they wore dark velvet caps, white shirts and trousers and radiated assurance. David Harris, the finest bowler, was a potter; Thomas Brett, a reliable fast bowler, a farmer; and the all-rounder John Wells, a baker.

The players did not over-encumber themselves with deference towards the nobility who helped to fill their pockets so handsomely. Once John Small - splendid batsman and fielder and accomplished violinist - received a gift of a violin from the Duke of Dorset. According to John Nyren, Small was not particularly fazed by this: 'Small, like a true and simple-hearted Englishman, returned the compliment, by sending his Grace two bats and balls'. For good measure, he also paid for the transport of the gifts. A star cricketer in the best team in the country did not need to bow the knee to nobility, no matter how genuinely philanthropic the gesture.

By the end of the eighteenth century, Hambledon's glorious deeds were over. Richard Nyren left the Bat and Ball Inn and the noblemen decided that Hambledon was too far away from the grounds of Kent, Surrey and Middlesex. Broadhalfpenny Down was left to the thistles and the centre of cricketing influence moved to London. Soon Lord's cricket ground became the dominant feature of cricket and has remained so ever since. No longer was cricket restricted socially and geographicaly, as the growth of the railways opened up England. Professional sides travelled long distances to play lucrative matches and cricket was the chief spectator sport in the country by 1850. The missionary zeal so characteristic of the Victorians meant the game of cricket spread swiftly to the far outposts of the Empire as well as the nooks and crannies of England. The Marylebone

agricultural land, controlled by the noble landowners whose large estates dominated the rural areas. The squires were their 'hands on' agents and the men they employed as gardeners or gamekeepers had an extra attraction if they could also play cricket. The noble lord's ego encompassed a good thrashing of a rival estate and he rewarded his workers handsomely for their endeavours on the cricket field. By the nineteenth century the concept of *noblesse oblige* was being loosened as the middle classes challenged the traditional dominance of the aristocracy. Hard work as the basis for self-improvement meant that entrepreneurs, industrialists and manufacturers grew in prestige. The aristocracy became more distanced from society and the country gentleman - the wealthy businessman enjoying a form of provincial gentility - became a major patron of cricket. The 'Muscular Christianity' beloved of Matthew Arnold fostered a desire to play cricket at public schools, to assimilate self-discipline and respect for civilised values, epitomised by the game. Cricket was deemed to be character-building among the upper to middle classes and by the middle of the nineteenth century, wandering sides were being formed to enshrine Victorian values. I Zingari was formed in 1845, the

cricket club had established itself at Lord's as the controlling agent of cricket, and has remained so. Never again could a village club like Hambledon challenge, and vanquish all-England as the game matured in the nineteenth century, with its rules common to all areas and no real advantage accruing to a local region. Yet it had been a collection of village cricketers who had respectabilised the game, giving it a shape and a format which has remained basically the same in the subsequent two centuries.

Eighteenth-century England was largely an

Quidnuncs in 1851 and Incogniti in 1862 - unashamedly elitist clubs, travelling England's green and pleasant land, playing against men of similar minds and social attitudes. So the squire's son might be lost to his village team at the end of summer term at college, because he preferred the company of his equals, to that of the blacksmith.

Country house cricket became highly desirable, played against the backdrop of the Big House, a timeless world unsullied by those who did not know their place. A.E. Knight, a professional player with Leicestershire, yet a man who would recognise the modern fad for upward mobility, positively drooled over country house cricket when he wrote about: 'The vision of sylph-like figures distributing tea and strawberries at four o'clock to tired players reclining in wickerchairs of ample dimensions.' A far cry from the prosaic scene often experienced by Knight in county cricket. The Kaiser's War destroyed that idyllic rural existence. Entire teams perishing in the mud of Flanders meant the days of the gentleman/cricketer were numbered, but in many parts of the country cricket is still played in front of the Big House. The fact that in many cases the team represents the nearest village is a major consolation for those who bemoan the passing of those elegant days of elaborately-organised, essentially private cricket matches. For the unsentimental, J.M. Barrie's desire to see a pavilion 'thronged with beautiful women and brainy men', his assessment of his own slow bowling as 'so slow that if I don't like a ball I can run after it and bring it back' evokes an age of insouciance that must have enraged the likes of Keir Hardie.

Away from the cloistered world of the striped blazer and the parasol, the game of cricket was faring very well in the rural England of Queen Victoria's reign. Stones were often taken out of the square, cowpats scooped up and the mower was invariably a few hungry sheep - but cricket had established itself in the nation's affections. A Hampshire schoolteacher, Mary Russell Mitford published a series of essays on rural life that left no doubts at all about the importance of cricket to a local community. She loved to watch 'a real solid, old-fashioned match between neighbouring parishes, where each attacks the other for honour and a supper, glory and half-a-crown a man. If there be any gentlemen amongst them, it is well - if not, it is so much the better'. Mitford railed against 'dandies showing off to a gay marquee of admiring belles' and extolled the simple verities of cricket where 'a village match is the thing - where the highest officer is but a little farmer's second son, where a day labourer is our bowler and a blacksmith our long-stop'. Parochial pride and self-sufficiency roar out of this Mitford assertion: 'We do not challenge any parish; but if we be challenged, we are ready.' One can feel the steady gaze from the Mitford eyes, and the quiet dignity of her beloved village cricketers.

By the dawn of the twentieth century cricket was a major social activity in England at all social levels. The poet and noted academic Edmund Blunden enthused about his village eleven, glorying in its mix of characters - the butler, the railway clerk, the vicar's gardener, the village schoolmaster and mine host at the Swan pub. Blunden called it 'a happy republic and one that had the chief intention of playing cricket'. Further up the social ladder, J.M. Barrie's advice to his country house players was unconsciously blasé: 'Should you hit the ball, run at once. Don't stop to cheer. If bowled first ball, pretend that you only came out for the fun of the thing and then go away and sit by yourself behind a hedge.' An advertisement in *The Stage*, the actors' trade magazine, captured cricket's enduring appeal in 1908: 'WANTED: actor to play Laertes and Lysander,

preferably a slow left-arm bowler.' Each week, *The Stage* devoted a page to cricket and the accounts of stirring deeds by the thespians in England's villages. By 1905, there were four hundred and fifty cricket pitches available in public parks around the London area - but more than fifteen hundred clubs applied to use them. Sonorous articles in the more portentous newspapers lauded the desire of the working class to escape the drudgery of the factory and enjoy cricket's soothing airs and that dedicated social climber A.E. Knight wrote: 'To provide greater opportunities for our national physical pastimes will also do more to rehabilitate the nation, to make men and women more wealthy in the long run than the decrying of athleticism as something which enervates a business nation.' Gad sir, the fellow almost sounds a Socialist!

While England's major cities continued to provide the labour that made the country the world's foremost industrial nation early in the twentieth century, life meandered along gently enough in the villages. The motor car was still a rich man's plaything so a village community remained self-contained, with its own professions and lifestyles. Even after the First World War, England was still a large patchwork of villages, whose inhabitants rarely travelled far. A man had a fierce loyalty to his particular part of his county, never mind his country and in that sense village cricket was a celebration of local pride. That philosophy shines through in the marvellously evocative book, *The Cricket Match*, written by Hugh de Selincourt in 1924. Now de Selincourt was a fair player (captain of the Storrington club in West Sussex for seven years), and in this book, the deeds of Tillingfold CC are clearly modelled on his personal experiences. The narrative surrounds the game between Tillingfold and Raveley, two neighbouring villages in the Sussex Downs. De Selincourt treats the local derby with reverence, as a form of benediction to village cricket and to the social mores underpinning life in a small community. Tillingfold, under the enlightened leadership of an artist, Paul Gauvinier, eventually triumph and after manly acceptance of their fate by the Raveley players, the titanic battle is mulled over in the village pub. A few hours later, Gauvinier rides home on his bicycle, savouring the pride of being the successful captain, imploring the day not to end. 'Even the cricket match was forgotten for a while as he looked at the blaze of colour which celebrated the close of the day. He rode slowly, lingering as at a majestic rite. The

whole vast sky glowed red and orange; the trees shone rosy in the reflected light which touched the hills. No breath of wind stirred the glowing stillness. His heart worshipped God and colour and life.' Anyone who has ever played village cricket and experienced the perfect day will relate to de Selincourt's intuitive, unashamedly romantic prose.

Today, cricket is thriving at club level in this country - despite countless other leisure attractions. Fishing is the largest participant sport in Britain, while jogging and swimming are tremendously popular but there are no signs that cricket is fading in significance. Quite the contrary, according to Keith Andrew, chief executive of the National Cricket Association. He estimates that about ten thousand clubs play cricket in Britain and that the NCA's 'Plan for Cricket' (in conjunction with the Sports Council) will safeguard the future of recreational cricket. Under its National Coaching Scheme, the NCA has seen more than fourteen thousand coaches qualify at various levels since 1980 and Keith Andrew is certain that the gospel of cricket is being spread thoroughly among the young, despite misgivings about adequate facilities. Club cricket has never been so strong, he says - but what about cricket on the village green? Here the waters muddy. When does village cricket merge into club cricket, with a resulting loss of informality and chivalry? Certainly the massive rise in league cricket means that the old days of bucolic fun on the village green are fading. We live in a harsher age; when a batsman gets hit on the hand, the modern fast bowler glares at the injured party without enquiring after his welfare. Batsmen rarely 'walk' during a league match, but will in a Sunday friendly. Village sides who only want to play friendlies find they have to join a league, otherwise they cannot get any fixtures. As a result, players in the leagues have become more streetwise while television's all-pervading influence has encouraged protective clothing, dissent towards umpires and an emphasis on winning.

It is a situation that perturbs Ben Brocklehurst, formerly an amateur with Somerset, now chairman of *The Cricketer* and guiding light of the National Village Knock-Out Cup Competition. Now in its twenty-first year, the competition was the brainchild of Ben and his wife, Belinda, who sat down and waded through the *AA Handbook* to discover how many villages could put out a cricket team. Culminating in a final at Lord's, the idea has been a staggering success and in 1992, more than two hundred disappointed clubs had to be turned away. More than six hundred sides are involved in the 1992 competition and the qualification rules are very strict - the village must not have a population of more than two thousand five hundred, no one who has played first-class cricket is eligible, there must be green fields on at least three sides of the ground and each player must have turned out on at least eight occasions in the past three years. The idea is admirable, to confine it to bona fide villages and keep the serious club sides out. There is no Man of the Match award, because the feeling is that the game is greater than any individual. Ben Brocklehurst monitors the trends very carefully; he is well aware that the lure of Lord's means that some sides are over-zealous in their competitive attitudes and that an unofficial transfer market operates, whereby good players change clubs in the hope of glory. Certainly he feels that the cricket has become more competitive in the competition's period and that some umpires face rather too much pressure from certain cricketers who are supposed to be playing for fun. Yet Ben Brocklehurst believes that, despite a few worrying behavioural trends, the game at village level is remarkably buoyant: 'There are more village clubs than in the past. The motor car has made travelling easier, there are now better facilities for shifting soil, so that cricket pitches can be created quickly. Despite the recession there is still money around to play cricket, a cheaper game than golf. There is more leisure time available and it's easier to play cricket overall if the desire is there. And it is. The teas are as good as ever too!'

It is a puzzling dichotomy that while village cricket appears to be booming, many villages are

dying out or becoming dormitory areas for the elderly or the rich. No longer can a village be economically self-sufficient; young people born there have to move away to work and they cannot afford to live in places that bring a gleam to an estate agent's eye. The farmer has had to streamline his operations and more sophisticated machinery means less work for human beings. So the old farmworkers' cottages are bought up and the process of gentrification gathers pace. On the one hand, the area of designated green belt in England has doubled over the past decade, representing almost fourteen per cent of the country's total land area - and yet the urban sprawl appears unchecked.

A gloomy prognosis of village life in the future was offered a couple of years ago by the Archbishops' Commission on rural areas. In its report, 'Faith in the Countryside', it noted that 'local village employment has declined; housing has become more difficult; schooling has been grouped with transport needed for it; local shops, post offices and halls have often been under threat of closure or have actually closed; local transport has declined to a point of uselessness in many areas; most doctors are based in local towns, with only a few using village facilities; and ultimately even the church seems to have followed the general pattern of withdrawal'. Mrs Thatcher, then Prime Minister, chose to bad-mouth the report, hinting at politically-inspired motives lurking under the clerical robes but it is hoped that her successor, John Major will indulge his passion for cricket by taking a hard look at the health of village cricket, as well as that of the inner cities.

As a devoted cricket fan, Mr Major will be well aware of the role of the village pub in the history of the local cricket side - and here again, the omens are not particularly favourable. CAMRA, the Campaign for Real Ale, says there is a distinct connection between the closure of the village pub and the decline of local activities. CAMRA's chairman, Roger Protz, himself a keen cricketer, says: 'The village community starts to die as soon as the local pub closes. Also the drink-driving laws lock you into your own locality and everything just withers away.' Roger Protz - who has just written a book on the village pub - believes that five thousand of them will close over the next five years unless the Government allows the major brewers to concentrate on profitable areas like towns and city centres. 'Those brewers who own more than two thousand pubs have to turn half of those pubs above that figure into free houses and they don't like offering other brewers' beer. So they sell off village pubs they see as unprofitable because they can get a nice price from someone who wants to turn it into a cottage for some rich yuppy. As a Sunday afternoon cricketer who frets if our match finishes before opening time, it grieves me that the brewers are selling off village pubs all over the place. Not every village side can afford a bar in their clubhouse, especially one that sells consistently good real ale, and the closure of the only pub in the village usually marks the death knell of the cricket club.'

Village cricket, just like life, is not what it used to be, but what is? No longer do the umpires shoo away the sheep from the square as they march with measured tread to the middle; the outfield is now mown with sophisticated equipment rather than a scythe; no blacksmith comes thundering down the slope in braces, snorting and pawing at the ground, bent on blasting middle stump back to the wicket-keeper. We view village cricket through a sepia tint, deluding ourselves that the rustic farm labourer still hits the wily parson's leg-breaks into the next parish, that foaming tankards of ale are quaffed with

the opposition, as they graciously acknowledge in the idyllic pub on the green that you were better on the day. Village cricket still retains its chocolate-box appeal because we need its escapist quality as we grapple during the week with profit margins, rapacious middle men, the obtuse procrastinators at head office or the bureaucrats intent on making our lives less fulfilling. We need our fix from the needle of fantasy, otherwise the utilitarian side of life holds sway. Despite all reservations, village green cricket remains the real version of our summer game, a rich seam of rural culture, a solid bulwark against a world that is moving too frenetically and in a country which is shrinking alarmingly.

The village game has thrown up immortal players through the centuries, including W.G. Grace and Jack Hobbs, and although today's tyro would probably be whisked off to winter nets by his county, then foisted with an agent and a sponsored car before he could vote - there is still the outside chance that we lesser mortals will be able to declare one day: 'See him - he once hit me for thirty in an over at Middleton Jockstrap. And I beat him first ball of the over with a beauty!' Allow us our dreams. Even the most clueless of batsmen has hit at least one ball in the middle of his bat.

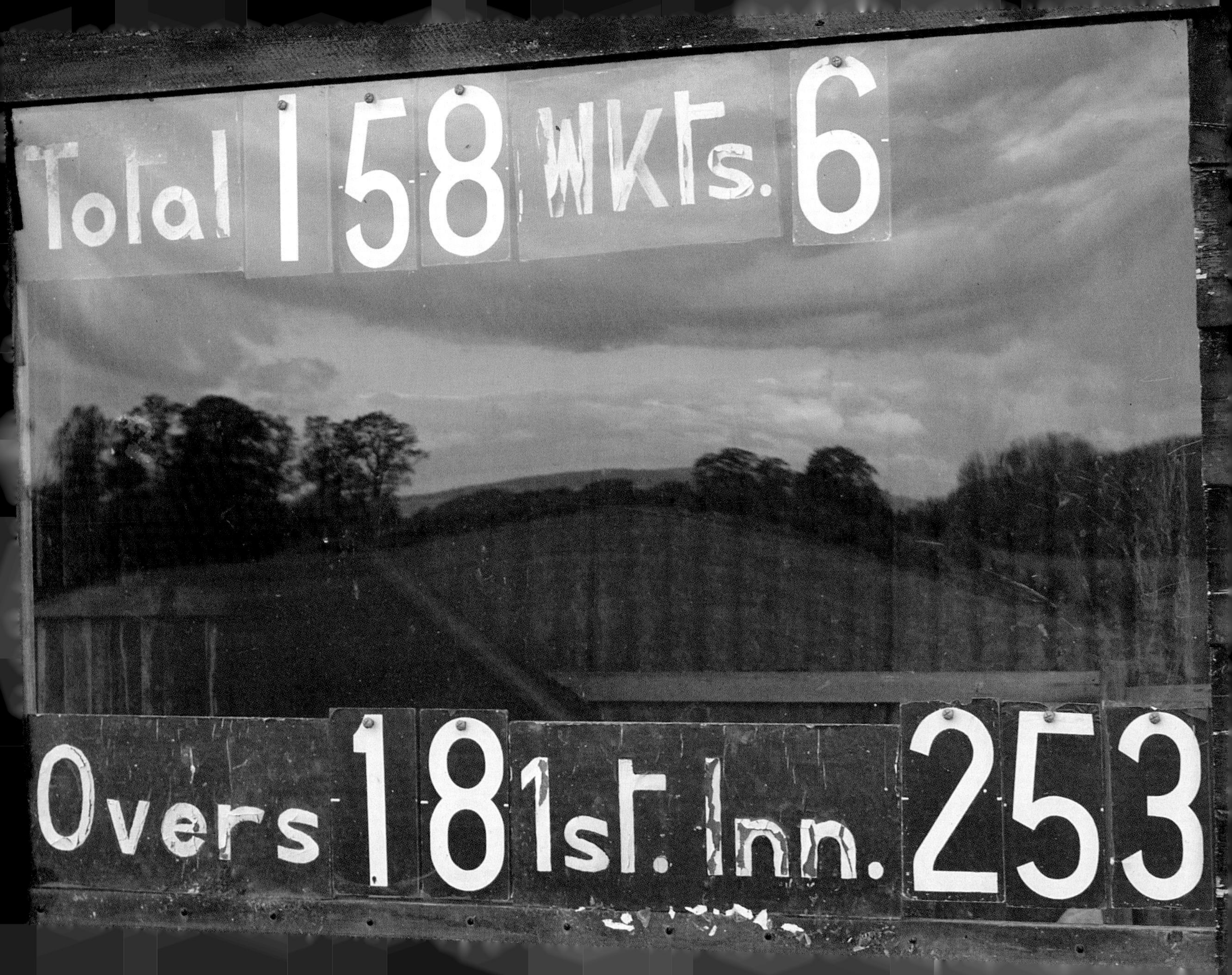
Total 158 WKTs. 6
Overs 18 1st. Inn. 253

Chapter 2

VILLAGE CRICKET GROUNDS

Adlestrop

BETWEEN A TRIANGLE of Cotswold towns (Moreton-in-Marsh, Stow-on-the-Wold and Chipping Norton) lies the tiny village of Adlestrop. The village school may have gone, and the pub, but the cricket ground remains a joy, half a mile away in Adlestrop Park. Set in seventy acres, the Big House that has not been occupied for more than forty years looks down on the cricket pitch. There is a lake a good hit away on one side of the boundary and inside the field of play, an oak tree - four runs and a 'dead ball' if it strikes the tree, and six runs if the ball goes through it.

The Big House was taken over by the Army in 1939 and used throughout the war but now, after years of neglect, it has been bought and a four-year restoration programme is in progress. Just four hundred yards away, the Worcester-to-Paddington railway line operates, although the noise is deadened by the line of trees. Until 1962, the station at Adlestrop was open, but then it became a casualty of Dr Beeching's axe and it perished, along with countless other rural lines. Yet Adlestrop station has its own place in literature.

In 1911, the famous poet Edward Thomas found inspiration as his train lingered at the station. Thomas, who was later killed in action during the Great War, proceeded to write one of the most evocative poems about the English countryside, containing the following lines:

'Yes, I remember Adlestrop -
The name, because one afternoon
of heat the express train drew up there
unwontedly. It was late June.
The steam hissed. Someone cleared his throat.
No one left and no one came
on the bare platform. What I saw
was Adlestrop - only the name ...'

Adlestrop cricket club has been going for a hundred years now and they only play friendlies, around fifty of them a season. They manage that with a hard core of about eighteen players, most of them with connections in the village. Only retired folk and commuters still live in Adlestrop, so the club relies on loyalty from those who have moved away. Eric Gordon, who has been associated with the club since 1938 and fixtures secretary for the past forty years, feels morale is still high enough to sustain a crowded fixture list, although the closure of the village school robbed them of several potential young players. 'But we keep going. It's surprising how many of our chaps play in almost every game. But it's a glorious place to play cricket and the pub we go to afterwards - the Fox at Broadwell, a couple of miles away - is delectable.'

Perhaps so many turn out for every game because they want to tax the statistical skills of Ian Hedges. Ian has compiled an exhaustive survey of every player's performance for Adlestrop since 1951, including how many fours or sixes, twos and singles each has made, and how many times they were out lbw or bowled. Ian's father, Derek, is perfectly happy to pore over each summer's labour - in thirty years, he has made almost 40,000 runs for the club and his son can account for every run.

Aldborough

YOU ONLY STUMBLE upon the village of Aldborough if you have made a special trip off Norfolk's A140 road. With some six hundred souls living there, Aldborough rewards those who still believe cricket can be sustained in a village. They've played on the green for more than a hundred and fifty years, with around thirty cottages surrounding the pitch. There's a Long Stop Cottage, First Slip Cottage and Second Slip Cottage.

There was a time when the team was made up of those who lived in the cottages on the village green, but - along with five shops, the saddle-maker, the blacksmith, and the Red Lion pub - those players have gone. Now there is just a general store, an antique shop, the Black Boys pub, and the cricket team is happy to sweep a five mile area around Aylsham to find players, especially at harvest time. When the parson, the doctor and the blacksmith all played, the occasional broken window in one of the cottages through vigorous strokeplay was viewed indulgently. Now, according to the team's doyen, Ron Dobby, some of the village community spirit has gone: 'Some of the cottages have been renovated and they're just used as holiday cottages. It tears the heart out of the village and we've had one or two complaints about broken windows. It's not that big a hit from the square but it didn't use to matter.'

Ron Dobby has lived in the area since 1922, when he was nine. He still plays occasionally for the village, purveying what he calls 'a sort of military medium', good enough to come second in the 1991 bowling averages for the club. When you have taken 3,500 wickets in your career for Aldborough - a hundred wickets fourteen times in a season - you still know enough to con a few young shavers, even if the arm is lower now!

Aldborough CC share the pitch with the village football team, and some of the younger breed turn out in both codes. They can still run two cricket teams in the Norfolk Alliance League, and for the sake of a dedicated club servant like Ron Dobby, they deserve a visit if the charms of Cromer pall one summer's day.

Ambleside

WILLIAM WORDSWORTH once lived nearby and the setting for cricket at Ambleside is surely worth a contemporary sonnet or two. They play at Rydal Park, just a quarter of a mile from Rydal Mount, Wordsworth's old home, and significantly, there is also a diocesan retreat for the Church of England on the estate. It is the perfect place for the contemplative nature of a retreat. Just a mile out of the holiday village of Ambleside, the ground is set in the basin of the Fairfield Horseshoe - to the west Loughrigg Hill, to the east Wansfell and to the north the three thousand foot Kirkstone mountain. So the ground is surrounded by hills, except to the south where there is a reasonable compensation - the glacial valley opens out to

Windermere Lake. It is serious walking territory and the cricket often acts as a welcome diversion for the rigorous hiker while sheep and cattle are always to be found in the vicinity of the pitch; indeed, the sheep are sometimes rather too curious about events on the field when play is in progress.

Rain is a problem for Ambleside's cricketers. They are the most northern team in the South Lakeland League, with the others playing in the Lancaster/Morecambe area, and the weather up there does vary drastically within a fifteen mile radius. They tend to lose more points than the other sides as a result at Ambleside, but at least they can see the rain coming over the hills and take steps to avoid the downpour. Because of the rainy area,

Ambleside's pitch is often pretty slow, but that is a small quibble in such idyllic surroundings. They have been playing cricket there for almost a century and manage to run two teams, and a junior side. Although some local cricketers choose to play at Kendal, fifteen miles away, Ambleside does pick up a few players from Windermere's Lake School, three miles away, and the teachers' training college. A few hotel owners in Ambleside also turn out and a marine radar officer's training college to the west of Windermere Lake is another fruitful source of players, from both lecturers and students. Useful for weather forecasters as well! A freelance local television cameraman plays whenever assignments allow; no doubt he would prefer to train his lens on the cricket and its environment, rather than chasing around the region, at the behest of his office.

With a small clubhouse and bar, Ambleside is one of the prettiest places for cricket in the Lake District. Over the last thirty years they have spread their wings, because until then the road system was too rudimentary for travelling very far, with any hope of getting somewhere by two o'clock on a weekend. Yet despite the necessity of going into a league, cricket at Ambleside still has a peaceful quality. And, in common with most tourist attractions, they even purport to have a haunted presence - a dog with three legs that allegedly haunts the road outside the cricket ground. Where would Britain's tourist industry copywriters be without the words 'allegedly' or 'reputed to be'?

Bamville

MANY GOLFERS love their cricket, and vice versa, but nowhere are the two passions more closely aligned than on Harpenden Common in Hertfordshire. Every Sunday after two o'clock in summer, the members of Harpenden Common Golf club have to yield to Bamville Cricket Club. By then, they must be through the fairways of the twelfth and fifteenth, so cricket can be played in the designated area. Both are par five holes, around five hundred yards, but peaceful co-existence ensures there is never a problem. Bamville always play away on Saturdays and they only pay for the use of their pavilion - to St Alban's Council, not the golf club.

Harpenden Common Golf Club was a racecourse at the start of the twentieth century - then came golf and, in 1932, the cricket club. The cricket team's first President, Jim Joel, was a famous racehorse owner and many workers from his nearby estate played for the club in its formative years. Those days are still recalled with great clarity by John Grant - now eighty, he was a founder member, groundsman, player and scorer.

All Bamville's games are friendlies. The square is small - what do you expect between two fairways? - but they work hard on it and it is acknowledged to be a good wicket. The players gather for nets in January at Hatfield (ten miles away), and the important decisions and exercises in nostalgia take place in the Three Horseshoes, alongside the golf course. They also have their own version of the

nineteenth hole; a clubhouse and bar for those summer Sundays.

Bamville's catchment area for players is the St Albans/Welwyn Garden City region. They pride themselves on being a small family club who do not need to enter a league to get enough fixtures.

The lure of playing cricket on a golf course seems attractive enough and the understanding between the two codes of sport ranks as a compromise in the best traditions of English amateur sport. There are no reports of any Bamville cricketer ever being disturbed by a cry of 'fore!'

Benenden

THE VILLAGE OF BENENDEN has a good deal more to offer than merely being the seat of learning for the Princess Royal in the 1960s. Just up the road from Benenden School, there is a splendid cricket ground where the well-heeled gels of sporting disposition can watch the chaps in white and forget about that crush on the gym mistress. Surrounded by minor roads and supervised by a marvellous old church, the game in Benenden is played on a classic village green. Here, in the southern part of the Kentish Weald, is where cricket was played in its formative years and the present custodians of Benenden Cricket Club are keenly aware of their heritage.

The most precise records date cricket at Benenden from the late eighteenth century, although the village green was used for bowls long before that. At the time the Bull Inn provided refreshments and it is still there today. The earliest reference to cricket on the green is in 1802, where the quality of fare at the Bull is described with as much attention to detail as the cricket. The great days of Benenden cricket were from 1825 for the next fifteen years or so, when two of Kent's great players also represented the village. Richard Mills and Edward Wenman were so outstanding that they took on an Isle of Oxney eleven in 1834 for a wager of twenty pounds - and the two players triumphed, even though they were the only ones who could bat and bowl. A hundred and fifty years later, that historic game was marked by a match between Eleven of Benenden and Derek Underwood and Alan Ealham, two great stalwarts of Kent cricket. That match was left drawn when rain intervened, just as the Underwood spinning finger was starting to twitch.

Benenden's players have been famous for their longevity. In the 1870s, John Wenman, Richard Mills and Edward Wenman - average age seventy-three - issued a challenge to another trio in England of the same age. They offered a sidestake of a hundred pounds but no one took up the gauntlet. Crowds of up to seven thousand were a regular feature of cricket on Benenden Green and money changed hands through bets and prize money every time a big game was played there. Fittingly, Edward Wenman and Richard Mills are buried in St George's churchyard, near to the green sward where their deeds made them famous throughout Kent.

Happily, Benenden CC has resisted the overtures from league cricket. The debate within the club remains active, but at the moment the majority view favours that of the more mature playing members, those who have enjoyed their cricket in glorious surroundings, without the imperative to garner points. They have never played in a league and a glance at their weekend fixture list confirms that they do not lack good opposition. Several Kent cricketers have brought teams there for benefit games, while the Lord's Taverners and the England Ladies' Eleven have also enjoyed the Benenden ambience. It would seem a shame to disturb the delicate mechanism of a happy club by embracing the idea of league cricket. Leave well alone, Benenden: be content with what you have. It's more than good enough.

Birlingham

AT FIRST SIGHT, the most striking thing about Birlingham's ground is the trees. It is a large ground by village cricket standards, but the mass of trees - beech, silver birch, tulip, and fir - help to compress the space. Until the gales of 1976, a massive walnut tree inside the playing area took pride of place, with six awarded if the shot hit halfway up the trunk. Yet Birlingham's ground remains a beguiling mixture of colours and shades. You drive in off the main road through the village, there is ample parking underneath the fir trees on the pavilion side and the jarring sounds of the motor car do not impinge on the sylvan calm.

Birlingham is set in the vale of Evesham, close to the market town of Pershore - and yes, the salad teas reflect the quality of produce afforded by the fertile Vale. The village is predominately a retirement area but market gardening keeps many of the players in work nearby. The area is strong in cricket sides - Pershore Town - especially so - but Birlingham keep coming up with good seasons. Both First and Second Elevens won their respective leagues in 1991 and they seem to be able to hang onto their best players, despite blandishments from other clubs. Senior officials speak warmly of the efforts put in by two key players (Martin Downe and Mark Shale), who joined as boys ten years ago, learned eagerly and well, and have stayed loyal. No doubt Mark and Martin have been influenced by the strain of continuity that runs through the club, exemplified by John Shepherd, obdurate batsman and canny captain who has been there for twenty-seven years. Even the scorer - Mrs Nancy Welland, whose brother used to captain the side - has been on conscientious duty in her little box since Birlingham CC came to Church Lane in 1965.

The club has been going for around eighty years, starting in a meadow behind the Swan pub. They owe their present idyllic surroundings to Major Harry Porter, who has leased the ground to them for a nominal sum. He and his wife, Anne, are very supportive of the club and once a year his President's Match is a notable occasion. The players are entertained around his swimming pool, the Porters lay on a sumptuous tea and their generous support of the club is always apparent. The Porters' large house looks down majestically on the ground and they confirm that the sight of cricket being played enhances their sense of well-being.

Although the Vale of Evesham soil is fertile and soft, the wicket at Birlingham is rock hard, thanks to regular applications of Mendip Loam. It is invariably dry and rewards the batsman. The clubhouse bar is there to goad the successful batsman into standing his round (and the groundsman is usually toasted by him and cursed by the bowlers!), and overall the facilities are more than adequate. Plans are afoot for larger dressing-rooms and showers but no one who plays at Birlingham ever departs muttering about poor facilities or lack of hospitality.

Bradfield

WHEN YOU STAND on the cricket pitch at Bradfield, it seems impossible to imagine that the proud, bustling city centre of Sheffield is just seven miles away. The village of Bradfield is set in the Loxley Valley, with the Peak District to the east, and the valley runs south into Sheffield. The cricket ground is flanked by three dams, with a river running at the back of the pavilion, linking the Egdon Dam with the Flask Dam. Rather too many cricket balls are lost in the river for the comfort of the club treasurer. They may be just three miles from the Derbyshire border, but they are canny Yorkshire folk and disapprove of waste; the batsmen should hit the ball along the ground, rather than go for glory slogs into the river!

They've been playing at Low Bradfield now for sixty years and the club is in its ninetieth year. High and Low Bradfield number around two thousand people and on a fine summer's day, there is always a goodly crowd watching the cricket, relishing the sight of the hills, the winding river and wondering who has won the Bradfield Jackpot, a fund-raising competition, shared between the bowling, tennis and cricket sections of the village. The three sports sections hope to raise five thousand pounds a year between them from the competition and the cricket club would be grateful for any cash to put towards a modernised pavilion to replace the one that has stood there for forty years. Any alterations have to be sanctioned first of all by the Village Fellowship;

in this part of Yorkshire, modern gimmicks like refurbishments have to go by the book.

Bradfield CC run two elevens. The first team play in the 'B' Division of Yorkshire Council's South Ridings Section (they do like long-winded sports competitions in God's Own County!) and the seconds are in the Sheffield League's 'B' Division. So many villages seem to play in Yorkshire: there are more than ninety clubs in the Sheffield League alone. So why does Yorkshire CCC fail so consistently to win any trophies every county season? (Discuss. Take a decade for research.)

In Bradfield, there is little work around, so the younger element drift towards Sheffield and rarely come back to play cricket. A year or so back, the club had to scrap the junior section, because the numbers dried up. The nearest school, which might have thrown up some youngsters, is three miles away at Loxley and there seems little prospect of young blood. It is something which saddens Bernard Wragg, the club's President: 'Our two youngest players are both about twenty. This isn't a built-up area, so buses are scarce and unreliable. If you haven't got a car, it's hard to get about and the kids have trouble getting to cricket, even if they want

to.' A far cry from the days fifty years ago when Bernard came along to the ground as a schoolboy, listened to the advice of his elders and eventually became captain. Where are the Bernard Wraggs of today in places like Bradfield?

Bridgetown

THE RIVER EXE plays an important part in the course of a game at Bridgetown cricket club. When you go there for a game, be prepared to have to take your boots and socks off at some stage in the proceedings. For the river winds all the way around the small ground and around six times a match, the ball has to be fished out of the water. Fishing nets are on hand for the less intrepid and although the exercise does little for the over-rate, it all adds to the uniqueness of the situation. The regular interruptions allow time to savour the setting. With the Brendon Hills lying to the north-east and the ground in the eastern part of the Exmoor National Park, a visit to Bridgetown cricket club refreshes the jaded urban palate. It is easy to understand what the club secretary and groundsman Doug Sherring means when he says: 'I've been playing here for thirty-four years and I love the ground and its setting so much. I drive JCBs for long periods in a working day and coming down here afterwards to relax is very special to me.'

Cricketers of a perfectionist strain should seek comfort elsewhere - it is a club for those in love with the very woof and warp of village cricket. You cannot drive up to the thatched pavilion; a wooden bridge must be crossed on foot, so the junior players are then deputed to carry the kit bag if the captain has any proper concept of the natural order of things. The bridge was reinforced last year after six hundred pounds was raised through the hard work

of the club. The pavilion is exactly the same as the day it was proudly unveiled in 1924, apart from a small room where the tea is made. Tea has to be taken outside the pavilion, no hardship with so many views to absorb, and there are no showers or flush toilets. No matter; Doug Sherring confirms that the side could play every day between June and September, such is the ground's popularity with touring teams. In the past it was common for some of the touring players to shake down in the pavilion with sleeping bags at the end of a hard night attending to the social imperatives after a keenly contested game. One London club side in particular spoke warmly of the quality of the water in the River Exe - ideal with the whisky they had procured earlier in the day. Such is the value of forward planning!

Once the game starts, newcomers have to adjust to the peculiar conditions. Set in a deep valley, the ground runs up on a slope on one side and newcomers always chase keenly up the slope after the ball - the old hands simply stand there and wait for it to come back to them. Local knowledge saves runs and energy!

Bridgetown runs just one eleven, they are in the West Somerset League, but they would rather play nothing but friendlies. Yet every surrounding village has its own cricket team and therefore they must play in the league, otherwise weekend fixtures would be scarce. They are short of players - youngsters are in short supply and seasonal work sometimes robs them of their players from the farming community - and they cheerfully eschew modern fads like nets. 'Just turn up and play - and enjoy it' is their credo and more power to their rural elbow. The square plays well, considering it takes fifty games a season and if it is slow, that is understandable when its proximity to the river is taken into account. An average of forty inches of rain a year in the area hardly contributes to a fast wicket, with the ball coming onto the bat. Such considerations preoccupy other clubs who are happy to play alongside a motorway, so long as they can have hot showers, see the ball get stump high and park their cars right alongside the spacious dressing-room. Anyone who plays at Bridgetown will agree the home team enjoy much the better deal. And the pub, the Badger's Holt, is only a hundred yards away. Whose turn to drive?

Brockhampton

THE PRETTIEST GROUND in the Wye Valley boasts no less than twelve different types of tree around the boundary edge - among them sycamore, lime, horse and sweet chestnut, scotch pine and three varieties of oak. Now that the showers have been installed at Brockhampton cricket club, it ranks as one of the best-appointed village clubs in either Herefordshire or neighbouring Worcestershire. One quibble would be the absence of a bar, but there are some excellent inns nearby. When Herefordshire came to play two county games for the first time in the 1992 season, that was the final accolade for a small club that has steadily improved year after year.

Brockhampton CC played its first game here in 1897 and they were greatly indebted to the patronage of the Foster family, who lived just around the corner at Brockhampton Court, now the site of a splendid hotel. The club's nickname is 'The Courtiers' and the influence of the Fosters has been great. No direct relation to the famous Foster cricketing family from Worcestershire, although club historians believe there is some distant connection. One of the Foster daughters of Brockhampton married Gerard Clay many years ago, and so the Brockhampton Estate eventually passed into the hands of Mr. Clay. Fortunately he was - and remains - an avid cricket fan, as befits a brother of J.C. Clay, the famous Glamorgan and England off-spinner. So 'The Old Man', as he is

affectionately called by Brockhampton's players, is now president of the club, fifty-six years after he first became involved.

In the early years of this century, Brockhampton relied on players who happened to work on the estate and at times the side was short of the quality now associated with it. Losing by three runs in 1903 after bowling out Perrystone for 26 must have taken a bit of explaining away, and in the same season they lost by 6 runs after dismissing Weston for just 38. Perhaps the outfield was too long in

those days! It is certainly now a batsman's ground; a hard, fast outfield, a pitch with even bounce and invitingly short boundaries behind either wicket. The club has put a lot of effort and time into preparing the square for good cricket. Twenty years ago, the square was moved around, east to west, so that fifteen wickets can be prepared, compared to the previous eight. It now costs about two thousand pounds a year to maintain standards on the square - that includes the cost of loam, fertiliser, mowing, electricity and, in an area that has suffered water shortages in recent summers, two hundred pounds for water. Add to that little lot four hundred and five pounds for insuring both players and the wooden pavilion, and it is clear tht Brockhampton must have a thriving fund-raising aptitude. Yet it is not easy to raise money in that area as the fixtures secretary, John Hudson admits: 'We're close to the borderline because there isn't a lot of work around these parts any more. Most of the farming land is arable and one farm takes up most of the acres around here - and yet they only need four workmen. It costs eight thousand pounds to modernise our pavilion and we were lucky that we had a few builders and electricians among the players to keep labour costs down.'

Yet many who leave this lovely village eight miles north of Ross-on-Wye come back at weekends to play, for the fellowship and the high standard. They run two senior sides and three junior teams, and after finishing second in the Herefordshire League in 1991, they entered the new Marches League with justifiable optimism. A stroll around Brockhampton is rewarding. Just around the corner from the cricket ground is All Saints' Church, a striking place of worship, one of only sixteen thatched churches in the country. It was built by the philanthropic Foster family.

There is more than one Brockhampton in the county of Herefordshire, so any lovers of village cricket ought to check the precise location before setting out. Not so long ago, mourners gathered at All Saints' Church to pay their last respects to a dear friend who had died in London. The body was being brought to the village in accordance with the deceased's wishes, and the mourners waited...and waited...and waited. Unfortunately the driver had gone instead to the Brockhampton near Bromyard, thirty miles away. The funeral service eventually took even longer than anticipated - but not as long as one of John Hudson's special blocker's innings. After 31 years playing for Brockhampton, he is still waiting to break in his bat.

Buscot Park

EVERY SUMMER, several cricketers playing at Buscot Park for the first time turn to their wives and children and say, 'Isn't this a lovely place?' They are right. For Buscot Park is the best type of ground for the family man who looks forward to his weekend game, yet hopes his family will not get too bored watching him try to re-discover his lost youth on the pitch. Importantly, it is a safe area for youngsters whose attention understandably wanders once daddy walks onto the green sward and finds himself fielding eighty yards away. The cricket pitch is in the grounds of Faringdon House, a National Trust property of unspoilt beauty, and although the busy A420 is near, connecting Swindon with Oxford, the cricket area is a long way from the traffic, so the children can play happily. When they are particularly bored, they can take a look at the Archery Club down by the big lake or gaze at the herons. Dad may wonder if he could ever land a massive blow into the lake from the middle, but no on has yet managed it - the lake is at least sixty yards from the boundary edge.

The ground is surrounded by lime, sycamore and poplar trees, with conifers on the side of the thatched pavilion. When the pavilion was re-thatched five years ago, the top part had '1892' stamped on it, but cricket was played earlier than that by the workers on the Faringdon Estate. No bar in the pavilion - not permitted by the National Trust - so they drink two miles away in Faringdon village. Buscot Park run two Saturday sides in the Wiltshire League and play friendlies on Sunday. They have about thirty players, a cross-section of builders, school teachers, printers and workers at the Rover car factory in Swindon, twelve miles away. The school teachers keep an eye out for young players but there is stiff competition for youngsters in the district, and Buscot Park know that is one thing they must attend to in the future. In the winter, they play in the indoor league in Swindon, which helps maintain friendships and fitness.

The club has its own historian, Martin O'Neill, their vice-captain. He has pored over the records since 1967 - before then, the scorebooks were thrown away - and Martin can tell everyone their precise career record for Buscot Park. 'Sometimes I pin-up how many noughts they've scored, but I wish I could keep a tally of the dropped catches!' Pride of statistical place must go to Dave Honeywell, the First Eleven captain. In the past twenty-five years, he has scored more than 9,000 runs with an average of 32, a fine performance, considering the quality of pitches he has to play on.

Some sides come from sixty miles away for league matches, and it seems no hardship to them. As

Martin O'Neill says: 'We get a lot of mums saying how nice it is to come here and not to have to worry about their kids getting into trouble. There's so much space for them to have a good time. And we put on the best teas in Oxfordshire!'

Canon Frome

AS YOU SIT on the mound watching Canon Frome play cricket you will look in vain for a house. The ground at Ashperton - near the village of Canon Frome - is isolated and rural in the truest sense. To the east, the Malvern Hills preside benignly; to the west, the market town of Hereford lies beyond a hill or two. The pavilion is built on top of a bank above the now disused Hereford-Gloucester canal. The tunnel is about three quarters of a mile long and the mound is an excellent vantage point to assess the battle between bat and ball. Behind the pavilion an oak tree that has seen most of this century spreads a soothing shade when the heat shimmers. This is cider country and the locals are proud of their Herefordshire roots.

Canon Frome cricket club began at Mainstone Court in 1938, with space found in the disused tennis courts area in front of the court, flanked by lime trees. After another couple of moves, the club settled at nearby Ashperton, down a lane near the village school. The 1992 season is a proud time for the club - after years of fund-raising, they finally came up with the necessary five thousand pounds to modernise the pavilion, with showers and flush toilets at last. Somehow the absence of such modern conveniences has never seemed to matter, as touring teams from as far as London and Cumberland would agree. The hospitality at the Hopton Arms, half a mile away, only serves to cap many a blissful day under the shadow of the Malverns.

One man who knows the club better than anyone is Ivor Hunt. At the age of twelve his prayers were finally answered midway through the 1938 summer when someone failed to turn up, and he got into his father's team. Fifty-four years on and Ivor Hunt is still playing for Canon Frome, a very useful batsman in the middle order, with an eye for the quick single that regularly shames team-mates half his age. Good enough to play for Herefordshire, Ivor opened the batting in the first team for twenty-five years with George Whittaker, the club's fixture secretary and a comparative stripling of forty years' experience at Canon Frome. Ivor has always been a great encourager of the youngsters, from picking them up and driving them to matches, to coaching, and his mantle has passed smoothly to the chairman, Phil Stock. Phil has excellent contacts at the local schools and thinks nothing of turning up at schools to coach cricket. It is due to men like Ivor and Phil that Canon Frome can boast three youth teams - Under-fifteen, Under-thirteen and Under-eleven. With a First and Second Eleven also, it is a major achievement that such a rural club can produce this kind of playing depth.

Canon Frome CC can boast many memorable days, including the one in 1974 when Rachael Heyhoe-Flint brought an England Women's Eleven to the ground. The occasional contact with the electric fence around the ground that kept the bullocks at bay galvanised the ladies so successfully that they thrashed their hosts by nine wickets. On a day in 1980, Canon Frome performed rather better - dismissing Much Marcle for 47 after scoring 419 for 6 in their forty overs. Victory by 362 runs, but if you are to be thrashed anywhere, it may as well be on a ground like this!

Cholmondeley

MANY AN OPPOSITION scorer has grappled with the spelling of the host side when they are at home in the grounds of Cholmondeley Castle. It is pronounced 'Chumley' and - another punctilious point - the estate is owned by the Marquess of Cholmondeley. Strange the nomenclature of the English aristocracy. Such attention to detail is a small price to pay to the Marquess for the pleasure involved in playing in the castle grounds, not far from the Cheshire/ Wales border.

The side was formed in 1886 by workers on the Cholmondeley estate and on one side, the castle (built in 1806) dominates the setting. The Cholmondeley family still live in it, although the castle grounds are open to the public on Sundays and Bank Holidays. Opposite the castle, twenty yards over the boundary, is a mere, linked by a bridge to a larger lake. It is a fair carry to the mere, but once the new ball was hooked into it after just ten overs and was never recovered. The old pavilion beside the mere is now used as a tea-room after the foundations were found to be insecure, but now a solid structure does the main honours on the other side of the ground.

Cholmondeley play in the Cheshire Cricket League, and just missed promotion to Division One in the 1991 season. They run two elevens at weekends and a midweek side. Officials at the club are well aware of the need to bring young players into the set-up, because there is little potential in the small village of Cholmondeley - until just a couple of years ago, there was no pub there. They trawl for players in a ten-mile radius around Nantwich and the schools are sent circulars, trying to encourage masters to recommend promising young cricketers to Cholmondeley before they are snaffled up by other clubs. Mike Bourne, who has been with Cholmondeley CC for thirty-five years, summed up the problem: 'We get quite a few in the ten-year-old range turning up for practice, and that is very encouraging. But we need to keep them interested for a few more years, until they're old enough to play against adults. At the moment we aren't getting many from the middle teens who could compete on level terms and a good standard.'

There seems little danger that the seventh Marquess of Cholmondeley will be forced to sell off his estate in Cheshire to keep the tax-man off his back. A recent survey by the *Sunday Times Magazine* estimated his family fortune at a cool hundred and eighteen million pounds (how *do* they arrive at that figure?) and with two lovely homes, around fourteen thousand acres and a highly-regarded art collection, the Marquess is managing to keep the wolf from his door. He is

also now the Lord Great Chamberlain of England after the death of his father in 1990. Keep an eye out for him next time the Queen opens Parliament; he is the one walking backwards in front of her during the ceremony.

Since he became the Marquess, the art-loving favourite of the gossip columnists has re-negotiated a lease with the cricket club to enable them to carry on playing in the serene shadow of Cholmondeley Castle. At a hundred pounds a year, the lease seems a snip.

Coniston

A WANDERING CONCENTRATION is definitely a possibility for those playing for the first time at Coniston. With such majestic scenery studded around the cricket pitch, the minutiae of pitching the ball on the spot or getting somewhere near a catch becomes simply that - fairly peripheral. Within a hundred yards of the pavilion, Furness Fells begin an ascent up to two thousand feet. Newcomers to the ground are often seen running up and down the gullies at the start of the Fells; definitely a ground to entertain high-spirited, active children. Yewdale Crags loom to one side and to the west, the Old Man of Coniston, at two thousand, six hundred feet one of the most distinctive features in the South Lakes area. To the east, just over the hills, lies Coniston Water, where Donald Campbell met a watery grave in 1967.

There has been cricket at the small ground just outside Coniston for more than a hundred years and the wooden pavilion carries that antiquity with a certain world-weariness. There is no electricity, just cold water, so the players walk down to the village hall for teas. There is no bar, but the Yewdale Arms nearby is perfectly satisfactory, an ideal place for committee meetings in the winter. As the club secretary Nigel Dixon puts it: 'We're an old fashioned cricket club in the right sense. I've been associated with it for forty years and no one seems to complain about the facilities when they come here to play.'

Coniston is home to about a thousand people and with the slate quarries offering employment, the village does have a fair amount of youngish folk still living there. Coniston Senior School still flourishes, so boys are coming through to play for their village side. Last winter a course for under-tens was held at the school, using a soft ball, and the interest shown was encouraging. Nigel Dixon, for one, feels the signs for the club's future have never been more positive. The Under-sixteen side contains a few promising lads and they seem to have no difficulty in running two senior elevens in the South Lakeland League.

The healthy supply of tourists in the area means the collection box sometimes rattles around Coniston's ground, and who can blame them? The club officials organise sponsored walks and other activities in winter, they tap up a few businessmen in the area for a contribution, and Coniston CC keeps going. In the first month of the season, the wickets are usually soft and spongy due to the change in the seasons, with water running down from the Fells into the Coniston Valley - yet what is the occasional waterlogged outfield compared to the glories of playing here?

Crown Taverners

SO MANY GOOD ideas are hatched over a pint or three in the pub. In 1970, a few cricket-mad regulars at the Crown and Cushion in Minley village, near Farnborough allowed their fantasies to run wild for a time and suggested starting up a cricket team. After all, there was a fair-sized green outside the pub, so why not put it to good use? So Crown Taverners was formed and now, twenty-two years later, they run two good teams. The First Eleven play in the Hampshire County Fourth Division, while the Seconds are in the East Hampshire Third Division. Friendlies on Sunday, when a more relaxed attitude can be adopted to the pre-match fare offered by the Crown and Cushion.

The ground is surrounded by large oak and chestnut trees and alongside the black-and-white timbered pub, the pavilion snuggles in - complete with verandah, patio, tables and chairs. You can watch the cricket from either the pub garden or the pavilion area. Although the clubhouse bar dilutes some of the takings at the pub, the two seem to co-exist happily enough. The occasional lofted drive scatters customers in the garden and more than one Bothamesque batsman has perished in the vain attempt to land a ball on the pub roof. Last season, Robert Hodgkinson managed it, much to the delight of his mother, Christine, the club's fixtures secretary.

Crown Taverners CC is a very popular fixture with touring sides from London and that is hardly

surprising. A clear run from the centre of London takes about forty minutes, thanks to the proximity of the M3 motorway. The link road to the M3 is just four hundred yards from the cricket ground, so that the horrors of the M25 are within fifteen miles. Yet there is no sign of contraflows or sound of lorries beside the Crown and Cushion - just the gentle hum of conversation that rises as the landlord builds to his relieved cry of 'last orders!' No wonder Crown Taverners can get so many players to turn out for them, with such ease of transport access. For the London-based cricket nut, its charms are obvious: you can work hard at the office in the morning, slide down the M3 at lunchtime and convince the boss you are out on calls in the afternoon. A good idea, though, to keep the carphone switched on and the recorded soundtrack of a busy motorway on hand, ready to be played in the background. A bit of a problem if you are fielding before tea, though!

Dumbleton

THEY'RE A SELF-CONTAINED breed down at Dumbleton cricket club and that's the way they like it. Dumbleton is a pretty, unspoilt village - named the best kept in Gloucestershire one recent year - but even though it nestles snugly to the north of Cheltenham and near the historic town of Tewkesbury, it is rarely tracked down by tourists intent on boosting the shares of Nikon or Fuji. There is no pub in the village and the average inhabitant would probably be able to name at least five members of Churchill's War Cabinet.

Dumbleton CC is a thriving club in its hundred and seventh year. Two Saturday sides, two on Sunday, a midweek team and one of the young shavers who are keener on emulating David Lawrence's galvanic leap and pace, rather than the subtler offerings of Tom Graveney, who lives just a few miles away. The name of Walter Hammond is still evoked regularly, but only by the elders as they reminisce about the great man's triple hundred for Gloucestershire before Hitler's War, when his batting partner for part of that innings against Lancashire was Vic Hopkins, a wicket-keeper plucked straight from Dumbleton's team by the county. Such romantic, meteoric promotion has gone the way of Neville Chamberlain's piece of paper and the tram. Yet there is still continuity with a less complicated world at this club. Ernie Lane has lived in the village since the 'twenties and at seventy-five, he still cuts the outfield. On mellow evenings in the pavilion, Ernie leads the sing-songs with his fine, clear voice.

The pavilion is a jewel. A fine, well-stocked bar, plenty of space for a long table that groans under the weight of a splendid tea and supper, intimate dressing-rooms, showers and - a godsend to harassed captains or nagged husbands - a pay phone. Up the hill there's an imposing hall, not for the scions of a famous family, but a holiday home for members of the Post Office Union. A vision of a classless society to delight that devoted cricket fan, John Major.

For a time in the 'seventies, Dumbleton CC was the strongest team in the area but then the First Eleven all got old together. A vigorous youth policy has transformed them in recent years, with the result that they now have a very good Second Eleven, full of gnarled old sweats who play for fun. The wicket drains well after being laid on a bed of gravel a hundred years ago, so that high-scoring games are a feature. Good humour is also a feature at Dumbleton. They call themselves 'the Dumblees', but they are not so clannish that they don't approach their matches with a generosity of spirit and appreciation of the opposition. Nominating a driver to stay sober is essential for every carload of cricketers that turn into Dairy Lane to take on 'the Dumblees'.

Eastnor

EASTNOR CRICKET CLUB lies in the dip between Ledbury and the Malvern Hills, but any suggestion that they are a Worcestershire village side is met with the shortest of shrifts. Peter Walker's local government reorganisation of 1974 may have spawned the county of Hereford and Worcester, but as far as the Eastnor players are concerned they are of Herefordshire soil and remain so. To them, Worcestershire players are 'townies', half-pint drinkers. It is no wonder Eastnor CC's attitudes are rooted in another age. Apart from the splendid pavilion (built in 1982) and the occasional car that tootles past the ground, there are no visible signs of the last part of the twentieth century on display. The church of St John the Baptist (built in 1852)

stands proudly behind the bowler's arm at the village end, the population has remained around the five hundred mark for a century and - proudly surveying the sylvan scene - Eastnor Castle remains reassuringly solid. It was built by the first Earl Somers in 1812 and when Eastnor Castle CC was formed in 1883, the first question asked of workers on the estate was 'do you play cricket?' Cricket on a Sunday and six days a week to work on the estate was their lot, and they were responsible for the upkeep of the ground. Water for the wicket came from the castle moat and the mowers were pulled by horses and oxen.

The timeless quality of the ground was underlined in 1973 when the BBC came to film Anthony

Trollope's *The Pallisers* at the castle. The book included a scene from a cricket match and as soon as the telly boys saw the ground, they knew that a faithful adaptation was more than possible. The current Eastnor players duly gathered at dawn one morning, submitted to fierce haircuts, enjoyed the on-location breakfasts and proceeded to enact the scene where Lord Silverbridge was caught on the boundary. Unfortunately the actor playing Lord Silverbridge was a negligble cricketer. After hurried consultations young Charles Taylor, fourteen-year-old tyro of Eastnor CC was drafted in as stand-in for the cricket sequence and acquitted himself with honours.

Although the population of Eastnor has barely grown in the last century, the club has little difficulty in attracting younger players. Liaison is close with local schools - the village one, praise be, is thriving with forty pupils - and a Colts side ensures the production line will not dry up. One of these days, John Taylor's leg-breaks will not harvest their usual crop of bemused batsmen and Jim Sandford will lose the touch that makes him such a prolific batsman, but, as they each celebrate twenty-five years with Eastnor CC , there is little sign of that. Players such as Norman Gifford, Basil

D'Oliveira, Bob Willis, Alan Ormrod, Brian Brain and Paul Pridgeon have all enjoyed lucrative benefit matches under the shadow of Eastnor Castle, but the village players are not the star-struck, autograph- hunting type. They respect the big names and like to help swell their coffers but they would not swap their cricket careers for those who appear in the first-class averages. When you've played a few years at Eastnor, you don't envy cricketers from anywhere else.

Ebrington

WITH SOME CRICKET grounds, you can just turn up and do yourself justice on the field without the need to know anything about the location. This is not the case with Ebrington, in the Cotswolds. If you want to avoid jumping in and out of a churchyard for half the afternoon, edge towards the umpires and engage them in lively conversation as your captain starts to deploy his fielders. That way, he will install you close in and put the onus for ball-retrieval among the gravestones on some poor, unsuspecting novitiate. Another tip - try to avoid fielding on the pavilion side, more than fifteen yards from the bat. There is a series of undulations in that area which test the strongest ankles and serve to make fools out of the most capable fielder. It is a

very short boundary on that pavilion side and the visiting captain should watch where the home skipper places his fielders. There is rarely a three to be had anywhere on the small ground, it seems to be either four or a single, so the fielders should either be right on the boundary line or very close in, to stop the attempted single and take catches. One more piece of advice, and it concerns three huge chestnut trees. If the ball hits the one on the edge of the boundary, that is four, or six if it is struck high up - but if it strikes either of the two that are inside the boundary, the batsmen keep on running.

American servicemen are responsible for the slope that makes fielding such a challenge. They were convalescing at Ebrington Manor during the last war, they started levelling out a field to play baseball on. They got two-thirds of it done, then hostilities ceased and they took their baseball mitts home to the States - leaving the potential for a cricket ground, complete with traps for the unwary. So Ebrington cricket club was born. They play there rent-free by kind permission of the Earl of Fortescue, a cricket fan who has turned out for the club and who lives at Ebrington Manor.

The pavilion is rudimentary and has not been altered since 1951. Until five years ago, the welcome presence of large trees in the horse paddock catered for any calls of nature, but now there is a portaloo - much to the relief of the ladies. Ebrington is not a wealthy club. They have around twenty members, most of whom commute from Chipping Campden or Evesham to play. They are in the first division of the Mike Procter Cotswolds Hill League and they do well to hold their own. It is a good wicket at Ebrington, despite the eccentricities of the outfield, and a good score is about 200. Their improvement in recent years is a source of great satisfaction to Ken Smith - player, vice-chairman, umpire and groundsman at the club since 1951.

Despite the unsophisticated facilities, they are a warm-hearted club who happily repair to the

Ebrington Arms after the match to mull over events. Mine host is a vice-president of Ebrington CC. Shrewd move that one: bring trade to the pub each weekend and then tap the landlord for a contribution to club funds. How else could sides like Ebrington keep going?

Everdon Hall

IF THERE ARE ANY sceptics who believe that rural cricket is now as conformist as the utilitarian age in which we live, they should take a trip to Northamptonshire and call in at Everdon Hall. The place reeks of history. At the top of a hill overlooking the Hall lies Castle Dyke, where Prince Charles's Royalist troops mustered for the Battle of Naseby. And those of a romantic disposition insist that underneath the cricket pitch is part of the secret passageway which linked the Hall to the church in Little Everdon, where the Crown's loyalists would gather to escape from the Roundheads.

The lady gardening over there is wearing a helmet - you were right first time. Anne Hawkins has been hit once or twice by a stray six and now takes no chances. This splendid lady would never dream of interrupting the game to complain about the bombardment, not least because her husband runs the side. The Hawkinses live at Everdon Hall and Captain Dick Hawkins presides over the cricket with just the right amount of genial despotism. At the age of seventy, cricket is now Dick Hawkins's sole sporting passion, after a riding accident ended his stint as Master of the Grafton Hunt. His hospitality is legendary - gin and tonics are dispensed in small goldfish bowls, not glasses - and he is a stickler for the proprieties of the noble game. Once a zealous fast bowler delivered rather too many bouncers against the R.H. Hawkins Eleven and was astonished to find himself the recipient of a

public rebuke by the worthy gentleman in front of his team-mates out in the middle.

Cricket has been played on the field beside the Hall since 1901 when Dick Hawkins's father decided to indulge his passion for the game. He was good enough to play several years for Northamptonshire when they entered the county championship in 1907 and he passed idyllic days of social cricket there until he died in 1930. Young Dick was at Stowe School at the time (good enough to take 100 wickets in one season for the school), and until 1948 the field was used by a herd of Jersey cows. The first full season was in 1951 and since then, Dick Hawkins has organised countless unforgettable days for those who like to play the game with a smile, a pronounced sense of sportsmanship and an awareness that the morrow will bring a hefty hangover. Around thirty games a season are played there. Everdon Hall has been host to some of the great English touring sides - Incogniti, the Rotters, the Crusaders, the Free Foresters, Cross Arrows, I Zingari, the Fantasians - and many overseas sides have gone away, spreading the gospel of a type of cricket many believed was lost at the outbreak of the Great War in 1914.

Dick Hawkins's players are selected as much for

their personal qualities as their cricketing ability. Among them, David Money, now seventy-two, and still the wicket-keeper, believes he has played up to seventy matches for each of the past forty summers. David, writer of atlases and books on China and Australia, has played in twenty-one countries. As an officer serving in India, he once had to arrest Mahatma Gandhi in 1942 after a passive resistance gathering headed by Ghandi turned violent. With characters like Dick Hawkins and David Money on hand, cricket at Everdon Hall is never dull.

Hambledon

BROADHALFPENNY DOWN near Hambledon deservedly rates an acknowledgement in the history of English cricket, but as we near the millennium, all is not what it seems down Hambledon way. The tiny pavilion is still there, and the Bat and Ball, where Richard Nyren chronicled the great deeds of Hambledon's players when they were the best in England. Yet today the villagers of Hambledon play their cricket two miles nearer to the village on Windmill Down. The Bat and Ball Inn is crammed with cricketing memorabilia, yet the locals do not patronise it; many come from the Portsmouth area, ten miles away, for evening meals and the tiny pub is usually packed out, without needing to worry about the needs of the local village cricketers.

On Broadhalfpenny Down, the Brigands play around thirty games a season. They are drawn from HMS Mercury, a training establishment two miles away, yet it seems the sands of time could be running out on that team. Mercury is due to close later in 1992 and it will be difficult to keep a team running over the next few years. On that basis the Hambledon Village Club applied earlier this year for the new lease, to enable them to represent the village once again on the historic Broadhalfpenny Down. Winchester College, who own the lease, granted a new, five-year lease to the Brigands instead. The village club has been told it can play a few Third Eleven games there and use it for

THIS STONE MARKS THE SITE
OF THE GROUND
OF THE
HAMBLEDON CRICKET CLUB
CIRC. 1750-1787

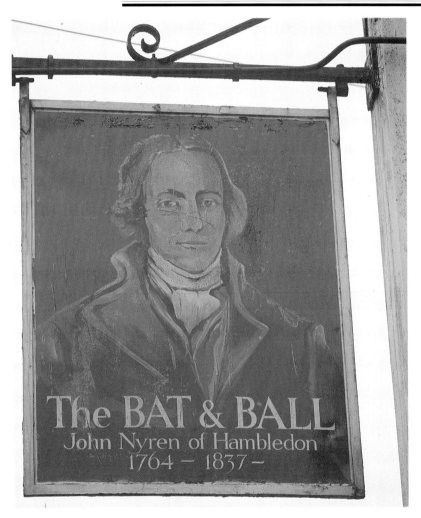

reverted to it. After all, Hambledon played there from 1750 to 1791, then followed Richard Nyren to a ground behind his new pub in the centre of the village. Broadhalfpenny Down was then ploughed up in the middle on the nineteenth century and the Brigands did not play there until after the end of the Second World War. It was Hambledon CC who organised the stone monument in 1908 to commemorate the club's contribution to cricket and now for historical reasons, officials of the club feel it would have been fitting for the ground to revert to the village side. They believe they are putting something back into local cricket. They have a wide catchment area for players, run three elevens and well-attended coaching classes for youngsters. The first team play in the Hampshire League's First Division and were beaten finalists at Lord's in the 1989 Knock-Out Final.

Hambledon CC know that the facilities at Broadhalfpenny Down are not good enough for league cricket and they realise that ownership of their own ground worked against them when they applied for the lease. Yet they are surprised that the Brigands feel they will still be able to raise a side once HMS Mercury closes. For the time being, Hambledon CC has to keep its powder dry but they

practice, but the club feels it could do much more for the image of Hambledon cricket if the lease had

have been encouraged by the suggestion from
Winchester College that a trust might be set up to
look at the future of cricket on Broadhalfpenny Down.
Sounds like the good old British answer to a ticklish
problem - appoint a committee to take the heat out
of the situation - but it is to be hoped that cricket on
Broadhalfpenny Down might one day revert to the

locals, rather than those connected with a naval
training establishment that just happens to be down
the road. The club would then be able to play third
eleven games and youth cricket there and satisfy the
countless requests by touring sides from overseas to
play a game on that historic ground. If that
happened, the Bat and Ball Inn would be even
busier.

Hawarden Park

SOME VILLAGE CLUBS are justifiably proud that a castle overlooks their ground, adding lustre and a certain dignity to the proceedings. Hawarden Park goes one better - it has two castles. One of them was built by Edward I to keep the marauding Welsh out of England, the other, almost a century old, is owned by Sir William Gladstone. Sir William, a direct descendant of one of this country's most illustrious Prime Ministers, allows the club to play rent-free in these splendid surroundings. Hawarden (pronounced Harden) have played on the Gladstone Estate for the past one hundred and twenty-six years, and they celebrated their hundred and twenty-fifth anniversary by winning the local Knock-Out Cup.

They also finished third in the North Wales League, where they run two sides, in the first and third divisions.

The pavilion is wooden, in keeping with a ground encircled by trees. The trees planted years ago by the Gladstone Estate workers are now majestic and dominating. It is a spruce set-up at Hawarden Park and the hard work put in by the likes of Malcolm Coppack, John Woodworth and Richard Penney has paid a handsome dividend. Around two thousand people live in Hawarden village, a quarter of a mile from the ground, but the club trawls for players in the Chester district. The seniors have indoor nets every winter and outdoors on a Friday evening in summer. Teams from as far

as Merseyside come for friendlies on Sundays and there are Chester and District League matches in midweek. The playing pool consists of around thirty seniors and some of the juniors are pushing them hard. The club started playing in the Under-Thirteen League this season and enough for at least four sides have turned up for nets on a Tuesday night. Such enthusiasm for the game from young players no doubt meets with the warm approval of Hawarden Park's benevlolent landlord, Sir William Gladstone - at one time Britain's Chief Scout. As every scout will confirm, you must be prepared, and it looks as if Hawarden Park CC are well ahead of the march of progress.

Holkham Hall

TAKE ONE IMPOSING Palladian house, add a lake, landscaped gardens in twenty-six thousand acres of carefully-tended land, a few languid deer and a cricket pitch - and the cricket romantic will sigh in contentment. That is the vista which awaits visitors to Holkham Hall, on the north Norfolk coast. Just one mile from Wells-next-the-Sea, Holkham Hall has long been one of the major tourist attractions of Norfolk. It is open to the public five days a week and the curious who stroll around to the back of the Hall will come across a gem of a cricket ground.

Holkham Hall was built for the Earl of Leicester in the seventeenth century and the current Earl happily allows the team to play there, rent-free. The cricket team was formed in 1843, for the estate workers or those who lived in the village of Holkham. Among the fixtures used to be one against the Sandringham Estate yet league matches were not encouraged, as they were deemed to be too serious. Happily that philosophy still survives today: the club play around fifty fixtures a season, all of them friendlies.

Sadly, the village of Holkham is contracting. Just a few estate houses and some retired people - the decline of agricultural work in the area has ripped the heart out of the villages. In the past twenty years, half the cricket clubs along the north Norfolk coast have folded. Holkham's club chairman, Geoff Mitchell, has charted the decline with sorrow.

'When I started with the team in 1949, we all came from Holkham village, either living there, working on farms, or on the estate. Now there are just two of us associated with the cricket club. We're a farming community and yet there's only about half a dozen I know locally who still work on the farm.'

So Geoff Mitchell and others worry about the lack of young players. With Norwich thirty miles away, and King's Lynn more or less the same distance the other way, there is not a dense population in the Holkham area. The club had advertised for young players in the local paper, without much success. The team is a complete professional cross-section, from barristers to bricklayers and some come to play from as far as Dereham and Fakenham, twenty miles away. Touring sides love to play at Holkham Hall and with the Victoria Hotel situated just by the main gates, it is always a hospitable fixture. The home players cheerfully deny that missing out on league cricket is a drawback; those of a competitive nature will still strain every sinew while the more reflective characters can relax and gain solace from the beauty of their surroundings.

If Holkham Hall CC just faded away, it would be hard on men like Geoff Mitchell or Bill Sutton, who still plays at the age of fifty and finds time to prepare around thirty-five pitches every summer. They have no difficulty getting fixtures, only players. Perhaps a strategically-placed notice or two in Holkham Hall might work the miracle? What cricketer with a soul would rather look at a chaise-longue than ask the umpire for middle and leg?

Honley

THIS IS NORAH BATTY TERRITORY, the area where BBC Television filmed the locations shots for their successful comedy series *Last of the Summer Wine*. Much of the filming is done at Holmfirth, a couple of miles away, but the good folk of Honley maintain the cameras show the only worthwhile parts of Holmfirth and that their cobbled streets are just as good. Yet the part around Honley Church often appears in the series, so local pride is assuaged.

There is keen rivalry between both villages in all aspects and Honley folk are convinced their cricket club is superior. The ground at Honley was bought by public subscription in 1928 and at four acres, it is one of the largest in the district. Indeed in 1974,

one Geoffrey Boycott deemed it good enough to bring a side to Honley for one of his benefit games. Sport is encouraged at Honley: just behind the cricket ground, a five-acre recreation field takes two football teams, and in the winter, the cricket club leases it out to the Huddersfield hockey club. The playing area is so large that the hockey players can use two pitches and still get nowhere near the cricket square.

They have a proud tradition of breeding fine players at Honley, the most famous being Alonzo Drake, who played with such distinction for Yorkshire from 1909 to 1914. After winning the local league's batting prize in 1907, Drake was called up by Yorkshire and distinguished himself in

a fine side. He was the first to take all ten wickets in a championship innings for Yorkshire, and also did the 'double' in 1913, but he was hampered by heart and lung trouble. Alonzo Drake died in 1918, aged thirty-five, at his home in Honley, the night after playing billiards at the local Liberal Club.

Honley play cricket in the Huddersfield League's top division, they run two senior elevens and three for the juniors, so the club's future is in safe hands after one hundred and forty-six years in existence. Ask Honley players if they play any Sunday friendlies and you are rewarded with a blank stare of incomprehension: they play to win in White Rose country. A double-decker pavilion in the style of a Chinese Pagoda, a tea room and bar all testify to the credentials of Honley CC. Last century, the players had to change in a canvas tent! Today's players and officials are all quick to point out that the ground is just five minutes drive from beautiful moorland. Once an area for the textile industry, only a couple of mills still function in Honley. As a result the River Holme is no longer polluted, and fish and ducks are in plentiful supply now in the river. Nestling on the lower slopes of the Pennines, beside the Holme Valley, Honley is a slice of Yorkshire village life, even though it is so close to the country's industrial heartland. And with Lancashire just ten miles to the west, the locals can always blame the bad weather on the enemy across the Pennines!

Tradition is important at Honley cricket club, and even the roller used by the groundsman bears testimony to that. When it was bought in 1949, it was named 'Jack' in honour of Jack Messenger, the club's faithful secretary for forty-one years. Jack died at the age of ninety in 1954, but the roller bearing his name is still wearing well. After seventy-one years supporting Honley Cricket Club, Jack Messenger above all deserves to be remembered.

Hovingham

TAKE ONE GLORIOUS stately home, add its owner who happens to be a cricket-lover and also deputy chairman of the National Trust - and you have an idyllic place to play cricket in North Yorkshire. Thanks to the Worsley family, the village team have been allowed to play on literally the front lawn of Hovingham Hall for a century and it is hard to imagine the scene has changed at all over the intervening years. The house was built of local stone in 1760; looking down from it, past the ground, is a glorious landscaped park leading to an ornamental bridge. On one side the pavilion nestles under a massive, clipped yew hedge, and some benches are strategically placed for enjoyment of both the cricket and the grandeur of the house. If the attention of third man or fine leg is ever going to wander, it will surely be during a cricket match at Hovingham Hall.

The house has been in the Worsley family since it was built and they have been loyal benefactors of cricket. There is a picture of a game in progress at the Hall, dated 1837, and evidence that a match was played there in 1858 between twenty-two men of Hovingham and an all-England Eleven, containing such legends as George Parr and H.H. Stephenson. In the century starting from 1860 it is estimated that more than a hundred Yorkshire county cricketers have played there, and in the early years of this century, the great batsman K.S. Ranjitsinhji brought a side every summer. The present owner, Sir Marcus

Worsley is keenly aware of these traditions. His father, Sir William Worsley, captained Yorkshire in 1928 and 1929, and was president of the club for thirteen years. Sir Marcus, a former Conservative MP and now Lord Lieutenant of North Yorkshire admits he lacks his father's playing prowess, although he has turned out for Hovingham: 'I think it is a very happy marriage between the House and the cricket team. I was born here and I remember with great happiness that cricket was played a great deal when I was a boy. The club is very good at fund-raising, they try hard to encourage young players to keep the traditions going and our privacy is respected up at the House. I very much enjoy having the cricket team here.'

Only about three hundred live in the village of Hovingham, and so the heroic efforts of the Second Eleven captain, David Skilbeck, are vital in laying foundations for the future. David scours the area between Malton and Helmsley and the second team is full of youngsters between thirteen and twenty.

One can only hope that stalwarts like David Skilbeck and the secretary Keith Elliott can keep the club going, as other leisure pursuits compete. Cricket at Hovingham Hall has to be one of the most aesthetically satisfying experiences in the English

village scene. One further vote of thanks to the Worsleys - the pub, the Worsley Arms, also in the family, is just a hundred yards away from the front gate of Hovingham Hall. It seems a satisfying arrangement for all concerned.

Hurstbourne Priors

THEY PLAY CRICKET on the crossroads of Hurstbourne Priors, with the road going one way to Andover, and in the other direction to Whitchurch. A couple of miles away lies Longparish and its village club, over-dosing on success and turning away good players. None of that for Hurstbourne Priors CC - they are proud to be village players and entertain no grandiose ideas. They have just one team, playing in the Winchester League - 'Sunday cricket with points' they cheerfully call it. Last season, they surprised even themselves by coming close to winning their league, but being bowled out for 44 in the final game did not leave much room for manoeuvre. Yet no dressing-room door was slammed, no tears were shed and within a few minutes, they were presenting themselves on the other side of the crossroads, to toast the season at the Hurstbourne Inn.

It is a pretty village, with the River Test flowing through, and the recreation ground for the cricketers is perfect. Many visiting players who have finally made it onto the green admit that they had spotted it while driving past and harboured ambitions to play there. It's been good enough for the cricket club since 1840. There is no running water or electricity in the pretty thatched pavilion - tea is taken in the village hall - but that does not seem to perturb anyone. Since 1989, there has been a chill in the

relationship between the cricket club and the parish council, after the council announced the outfield was not being maintained properly in its opinion. In turn, the club was unhappy that the council was renting out the green to other sides. The deeds of the ground decree that a team must always represent the village, the club must now pay thirty pounds a game and five pounds for the use of the village hall to the parish council. Seems a shade harsh on the cricketers, but the dispute has only served to stiffen their sinews. Says Geoff Rampton, the secretary: 'We had a couple of lean years, but we're fighting back. A lot of us have roots in the village, even though we don't live there any more. Some of our best players have gone off to Longparish, but we don't begrudge them their success. They're a very good outfit, but we like the way we play the game. No one who ever comes here to play against us ever complains about the facilities or the wicket, so I reckon we must be getting it about right.'

Hopefully, peace has broken out between Hurstbourne Priors CC and the parish council. If all else fails the club could always look a couple of miles to the north-east and enlist the advocacy of Whitchurch's most famous son. Lord Denning has tilted at bigger windmills that a parish council.

Ingham

TWEAK THE COMPASS a couple of points to the east and there is nothing between Ingham and the Arctic, but that does not mar the aesthetic pleasure of cricket at Ingham. Officials believe theirs is one of the prettiest grounds in Norfolk and they point to an independent witness for corroboration. Anyone idly flicking through the 1992 calendar of a famous tyre company will come across a painting of Ingham's ground, and it is hard to demur. The ground is encircled by pine, elm, oak, ash and sycamore, and although the storms of 1989 caused some damage, a handsome grant from North Norfolk District Council means the former glories will eventually be fully restored.

Ingham celebrated its centenary a couple of years back in some style, with a trip to the Far East when they played in Hong Kong and Bangkok. They are a cosmopolitan club, picking up players from as far afield as Earl's Court and Australia.

Ingham are also a very sociable club. Their reputation tends to precede them, as more than one good player from the region has said: 'I'd love to play for you, but those drink-drive laws are a worry.' Ingham's players pride themselves on approaching their cricket in a positive fashion. As their secretary, Brendon St. John Dwyer says: 'We would rather lose narrowly going for fifteen points for a win, than block it out for a draw and risk just picking up one point.' That aggressive style occasionally backfires: Ingham know what it's like to be dismissed for 160, having been 140 without loss. On the other hand, they once made 220 for 9 declared, after being 60 for 9. One Tracy Moore was the hero that day with a hundred, and on many other occasions he has been the star with his brisk medium pace. Tracy took a stack of wickets for Norfolk and has captained the Minor Counties.

Ingham run two teams, plus an Under-sixteen section. Their First Eleven play in the county's strongest league - the Norwich Junior Alliance - and they have won that seven times since 1975. They also won the Knock-Out Cup three times in the 1980s. Continuity is important: take the Borrett family. Jack played for Lord's Taverners for a number of years, was President of Norfolk and player/groundsman at Ingham for longer than he cares to remember. His son, Paul now tends the ground and captains the Second Eleven, while his thirteen-year-old grandson Christopher shows every sign of carrying on the good work.

This summer Ingham pulled off a rather useful signing without any undue effort. Rodney Bunting, the Sussex all-rounder left the county in 1991 and came back to Norfolk. A King's Lynn lad, he approached Ingham to see if he could play for them. The club's officials thought about the offer for all of

a second, agreed they could probably fit him in for an occasional game in the seconds, and graciously acceded to Rodney's request. The strength of Ingham Cricket Club is that he would have to fit into *their* way of approaching the game, both on and off the field.

Langleybury

ONE OF THE MODERN cricket miracles of England's countryside is the way the intrusive fumes and noise of motorways seem to be anaesthetised by the time they reach the village green, just a field or two away. Langleybury is a classic example. The A41 Watford to Hemel Hempstead road goes right past the ground, while a quarter of a mile away runs the M25 - yet trees and the pavilion shield the players from the A41 and no one on the pitch would know that the M25 and London were so near. Perhaps God is a groundsman after all.

One of the glories of cricket on Langleybury Green is the church, clearly visible from the middle, and in its own way, responsible for the cricket club. Forty years ago, the vicar Canon Ron Martin, a fine player at Cambridge University when younger, felt that the village of three hundred or so needed a cricket team. Alan Bunn, a former RAF fighter pilot and then member of the parish council agreed and between them, they made it all happen. Canon Martin is dead now but Alan is a life member and trustee of the ground and has watched the club's development with quiet satisfaction. Just two miles away are Abbot's Langley CC and King's Langley CC (both over a hundred years old) and it is a fine achievement to set up another club in an area full of cricketers. Langleybury play in the Hertfordshire Competition on Saturdays, the Home Counties League on Sundays and they also have a third team for friendlies. Several of their youngsters have played for the County Colts, and the junior side keeps turning out some bright prospects. On five occasions Langleybury have reached the semi-finals of the National Village Knock-Out Cup. Chris Young has been a player with Langleybury since 1958 and he has seen the standard rise steadily. 'In my early days we used to have a job getting eleven men, never mind those who could play. One or two of them would just stand in the outfield and then help make the tea. Now it's all so much more competitive and the smell of linament has been replaced by the smell of aerosols. I still love it, and I want to keep playing. My son turns out now and then, which gives me pleasure. It's still the best game there is.'

Langleybury CC has to work hard on fund raising. It cost three thousand pounds a few years back to repair the roof of their pavilion and they were grateful to the current England soccer manager, Graham Taylor who came over with his players when he was at Watford to boost the club funds at a Sportsmen's Dinner. They now have their own bar in the pavilion and after the old one was burnt down, the reconstructed pavilion is sufficient to their needs. Several trees have been planted around

the boundary edge to buttress the splendid array of lime and beech. Hopefully Chris Young will still continue to accumlate the minutiae, newspaper cuttings and old scorebooks of Langleybury's deeds since 1952. A solicitor, Chris also has an archivist's eye for detail and his history of the club will be worth reading. Only a cricket fanatic would have an address like 'The Wickets'. Could be worse - Chris might have called his house 'Dunbowling'!

Leigh

THIS IS ONE OF the great old Kentish clubs in the classic village green position. Leigh (pronounced Lye) has seen cricket for hundreds of years. Earliest records suggest games in the area from 1700 onwards, although there is evidence that cricket might have been played there at some time in the previous one hundred and fifty years. The first recorded match on the village green at Leigh came in 1774. The Bat and Ball Inn has served the villagers since the early part of the eighteenth century, which indicates that cricket had been an integral part of Leigh life for some time before that. With cricket balls being made at nearby Penshurst long before 1700, it is a reasonable premise that the game was also played in the local village at the same time. Leigh cricket club is splendidly, robustly and proudly *old*.

St Mary's Church overlooks the cricket on the green at Leigh, a village of around fifteen hundred people, with a strong agricultural connection. The green is surrounded by chestnut trees, so it is understandable that the club tie features a tree and '1700' as the motif. The club play in the Kent Village League and run two sides. Several youngsters are coming through; they have about a dozen midweek evening matches a season and coaching is available each Sunday morning.

They are justifiably proud of their cricketing history at Leigh, at the way the club has kept going in adverse circumstances. Eric Batchelor, the club's president and treasurer has been associated with Leigh CC since 1937 and he recalls cricket being played there regularly during the last War, despite the presence overhead of Messerschmitts and Spitfires. An Army barracks nearby provided a host of able-bodied men anxious to play some sport and Leigh's village green was the perfect location. Yet life on the green was a good deal more turbulent at the end of the eighteenth century, when they attempted to play cricket on Leigh Fair Day. That was often a pretty combustible affair, with traders, amusement stalls, clowns, musicians and even the occasional performing bear. Mix in unlimited drink, the presence of some commercially-minded ladies of dubious virtue, and hot weather, and one can understand why the cricketers used to dread Leigh Fair Day. How can a chap concentrate on his forward defensive when all that wenching is going on just behind the bowler's arm?

There is one pleasing reminder of the early times of Leigh CC - and it is provided by the Duke family. They were connected with the club for more than a century and manufactured cricket balls close to the village. Today Duke's cricket balls are used in Test and county matches and the

name of John Duke is stamped on them. John played for Leigh until 1854 and the line of Duke cricketers finally dried up in 1924. So the next time you are thrown a cricket ball stamped 'Duke', pause for a moment or two and savour the sense of continuity that the game on a Kentish village green still offers all around the world.

Linton Park

ONE OF THE DOYENS of Linton Park cricket club put it rather well a year or two back: 'The trouble at Linton is that it spoils you for playing anywhere else.' For more than two hundred years, cricket has been played on the Linton Ridge, overlooking the Kent Weald. It is a classic hilltop ground, with the stumps pitched on the flat dome of the hill and the land sloping away past the hawthorn bush on the midwicket boundary. There are giant lime and copper beech trees around the ground and until the gale of 1987, the entrance to the playing area was spectacular. Driving a quarter of a mile off the main road from the village of Linton, you would pass through a tunnel of trees, then just come across the green sward. A breathtaking sight

for the newcomer. Such is the tradition, however, that it is fair to assume that unique tunnel effect will be restored in the course of time.

Linton's pavilion also underlines this feeling of timelessness. Recently showers and a kitchen have been installed but very little else about it has been altered this century. That is the way they like it at Linton. They cherish the fact that not a house can be seen from the ground, that there is no sound of passing traffic. The only ear-shattering sound you will hear on this ground is the appeal of a convinced bowler. Even the village of Linton has changed little over the years. With just six hundred people in the village, there has been no increase in building or population since the last war. Only the cricket team's playing fortunes have progressed.

Linton Park is steeped in cricket history. The first game was played here in 1787, when Sir Horatio Mann, one of the great cricket patrons, organised matches with wagers of a thousand guineas a side going to the winners. The ground then passed to the Cornwallis family and the fifth Earl became a notable benefactor. His grandson improved the ground even further and played many seasons, bringing some famous players for the cricket weeks.

Dynasties are common at the club. Tom Peach was the first of his family to play there. To date, nine of the dynasty have played for Linton Park, including Alan (who played for Surrey), Charlie (Kent) and Tom's grandson, John Thirkell. John is known today as 'Mr Linton Park' and, after more than sixty years' service there, he cannot argue with the title. He is still secretary. John's sons have also been captain and vice-captain of the two elevens and with a couple of grandsons showing promise, the future of the Peach dynasty seems as secure as the club's fortunes.

Linton Park play in the Kent Invicta League. They won it in 1991 but their proudest moment in recent seasons was victory at Lord's in 1978 in the National Village Knock-Out Cup Final. John Thirkell was

there to see his son, Nigel play the crucial innings. Do not bet against them winning the cup at Lord's once more. More importantly, with such men as John Thirkell keeping a paternal eye on the club, there will be no danger that Linton Park will become too trendy. The ghosts of the Manns, the Cornwallises and the Peaches would not tolerate such insensitive excesses.

Longparish

FEW VILLAGE CRICKET GROUNDS in the country can rival Longparish for success on the field and aesthetic beauty. Despite the demise of several Dutch Elm trees in the 1987 hurricane that swept the south of England, the ground in the centre of the Hampshire village is immaculate. It is set in a conservation area and thus any work to be done on the cricket ground must be in keeping with the overall quality. After seventy years, the delightful thatched pavilion is on borrowed time. Senior officials at the club feel facilities must be improved, and when the time comes for rebuilding, many will be anxious to ensure the new pavilion blends in with the existing environment. The

alterations will cost a cool thirty-five thousand pounds and although it is hoped the new pavilion will be installed for the start of the 1993 season, there are some at the club who would be perfectly happy with renovation, rather than gutting of the old building. Ambition can be a turbulent influence on something as conservative as village cricket.

The problem - if indeed it is one - for Longparish CC is that it has become a very successful club over the past twelve years. For a village of around a thousand people - dubbed Longparish because it is literally one long street - the cricket team can be justly proud of its efforts. They have reached the final of the Knock-Out Cup twice at Lord's (winning in 1987), and carried off the Hampshire League four times. They have also monopolised the local indoor cricket league and seem to be the side everyone wants to beat. Even when they put out a weakened team for a midweek evening match, the players of Longparish feel they know what it must be like for Liverpool in soccer; they are there to be shot at. Players from other local clubs approach Longparish to see if they can turn out for them, so there is no problem of selection. Although eight of the side that lost in the 1980 Lord's final hailed from Longparish, times have changed in the intervening years. The village is full of desirable residences near the River Test, within easy commuting distance of many towns and cities, and once the estate agents get to work on their glossy, hyperbolic brochures, the escalating prices of property drive the young families out of a place like Longparish. The fate of many a picturesque English village near to a motorway.

Despite the absence of young blood in Longparish, the fortunes of the cricket club look certain to wax, rather than wane. There has always been a strong cricketing tradition in Longparish. John Woodcock, the erstwhile cricket correspondent of *The Times*, was born, and still lives in the village, and he has brought players of the calibre of Colin Cowdrey, Richie Benaud, Len Hutton, Denis Compton and Frank Tyson to the ground for charity matches. The days when the locals would goggle at such legends have long gone, sadly. When your own village players have appeared in two finals at Lord's in just seven years, you tend to get a shade blasé about propping up the bar with old Compo.

Lowther

THE PLAYERS OF Lowther cricket club certainly enjoy visual compensations for the lack of facilities on their ground on the fringe of the Lake District. The pavilion may be basic - no electricity, no showers, just a tap - but the views from it are superb. You look down the Eden Valley to the Pennines and on another side, there is Cross Fell, all three thousand feet of it. There is woodland all around the ground and it is hard to believe that with Ullswater two miles to the west, the M6 motorway is just half a mile away.

They pride themselves on being part of the grass roots of cricket at Lowther, a small village four miles south of the market town of Penrith. They can only run one team (just fifteen playing members), and a fair proportion of the squad are teenagers. They have at last acquired a mower, but the sheep are allowed on during the winter to keep down the grass. Stones and shingles periodically pop up from the surface of the square, but at least the ashes have settled underneath after sixty-five years, so the bounce is even. There is no bar in the tiny pavilion, but the Lowther Castle pub is just half a mile away. None of this matters. Lawrence Titterington - secretary, treasurer, teaboy and still an occasional Sunday player after more than thirty years with Lowther - has it exactly right: 'It's pure, authentic village cricket here. We play to enjoy the game and our surroundings. I'm not sure it matters all that much that the outfield could be smoother or the

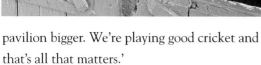

pavilion bigger. We're playing good cricket and that's all that matters.'

They are no slouches, either. Holders of the Eden Valley Cup (25 overs a side), they hold their own in the Eden Valley League. There has been cricket at Lowther since 1926, courtesy of the Lonsdale family. One of the earlier Lonsdale Earls provided the famous belts for those of a pugilistic bent, and the present Earl Lonsdale allows the club to play on his land for a pound a year. There is an oak tree inside the playing area and four runs are credited if the ball hits the tree. Yet a whole season can go by without the tree being hit, which perhaps summarises the style of batmanship at Lowther. The tree is at fine leg and long-off for the right-hand batsman, yet the ball never seems to go in that direction. Does that mean the leg-glance and the lofted off-drive are rarely seen on the playing field of Lowther CC? Perhaps the wicket is too slow and the nurdle to third man or the nudge off the legs are more productive shots. Shame; the grandeur of the setting deserves a few lofted drives over long-off's head.

Lustleigh

A LOVELY LITTLE GROUND in a lovely little South Devon village, next to Dartmoor. A perfect area for hikers and pony-trekking, the ground is surrounded by trees - beech, alder, chestnut and oak - with hills on one side and Dartmoor on another. It is set in the Wrey Valley and the River Wrey meanders along one side of the boundary. It is a small ground - just fifty yards from the middle - so a big hit easily clears the river and lands in a field. The Cleave pub is just twenty yards from the dressing-room, so it's hard to know what else a cricketer could want from this delightful ground.

Lustleigh village houses about three hundred people, to the north-west of Newton Abbott. It is dotted with holiday homes and the bulk of the regulars in the village are self-employed, with no desire to move to more frenetic lifestyles. The aspirations of the cricket team mirror that relaxed approach: they prefer playing in friendlies because they are a mixture of the good, the indifferent and the useless. As a result everyone seems to get a bat or bowl and they all feel the day has not been without purpose if the players can at least be tested in action. They play in the winter indoor league and the Knock-Out Cup against teams they have known for years, but the overall impression of Lustleigh CC is of a group of players who know their limitations and would be happy to jog along in the same groove. The club celebrated its fiftieth

anniversary in 1989 and it was wholly appropriate that the guest speaker at their dinner was Vic Marks, a proud Somerset man of farming stock who never lost sight of the fact that it was only a game throughout his fine career.

Lustleigh run just one eleven and towards the end of the season, they face a few manpower problems, as some of their young cricketers answer the call of football, four miles away at Moretonhampstead or Bovey Tracey. The cricket club travels as far as North Devon and as far south as Plymouth (thirty miles away) but they prefer to play at home. Their fixtures secretary confirms that many a side lobbies for an invitation to play at Lustleigh.

They encourage families to come and enjoy the cricket at Lustleigh and the captain, Steve Wright sets a good example in that direction. His two brothers, Shaun and Michael play under his command, and so does his father, Courtney. That's not the end of the Wright connection - Steve's mum, Irene, makes the teas and his wife, Tina, is the club secretary. One hopes for the sake of Lustleigh CC's future that Steve and his brothers disapprove of vasectomies.

Lynton and Lynmouth

EVERY CRICKETER HAS at some stage wanted to throw himself off the nearest cliff after a particularly frustrating performance, and at Lynton and Lynmouth cricket club, that can be arranged. The ground is set in a stunning position, almost an amphitheatre. The Valley of Rocks is a famous beauty spot at the edge of the West Exmoor National Park and the tiny ground nestles in front of the escarpment. If the lungpower can take the strain a climb up the rocks is highly rewarding - a marvellous view out over the Bristol Channel one side, stunning parkland the other way, with a bird's eye view of the cricket down below.

Back on terra firma, the thatched pavilion is almost built into the rocks. The boundaries are very short, particularly on the side of the road that ferries tourists to the Valley of Rocks. The local cricketers have long been used to the sight of Americans and Japanese tumbling out of coaches and snapping away with their cameras, as Lynton and Lynmouth enact this strange sport which has captivated English folk for centuries. The coach drivers are rather more aware of potential damage from a flying cricket ball, and they negotiate the drive past the ground with due despatch!

The combined population of the two villages is only two thousand, so at times the club has problems finding players, especially now that it has two sides in the North Devon League. The cricket struggles for money, so membership is twenty pounds a season and five pounds for the juniors. Without the sponsorship of each home match by Clair and Tony Vickery, the cricket club would be in dire straits. The fact that the Vickerys run the local pub - the Exmoor Sandpiper Inn - and that Tony plays for Lynton and Lynmouth is a highly satisfactory arrangement for all concerned. Vigorous fund-raising by the vice-presidents also helps to keep the club afloat, but it is not easy in such an isolated area.

Understandably, this is one of the most popular grounds in the area for touring sides. The Birmingham Diocesan Clergy come down every summer, no doubt some of them communing with the Almighty during the game on top of the rocks, while a bedraggled bunch of cricket writers from the national newspapers are rather more dedicated to boosting the bar profits of the Exmoor Sandpiper Inn. The cricket writers tend to have sketchy memories of their annual jousts with Lynton and Lynmouth CC, but as one, they tick off the days each summer before pitching up at the Valley of Rocks. Their advocacy in persuading their sports editors that an important cricket story is about to break in North Devon is almost as admirable as the creative expenses claims that follow the trip.

Although Lynton and Lynmouth CC. love to play

host in midweek, they do have trouble raising a side at times, so they have to beg and borrow from other local teams. The club happily admits that tourists to the area are welcome to play at short notice - so pack the cricket gear as well as the suntan cream.

Manderston

THEY DO A MARVELLOUS cap at Manderston cricket club. A splash of colours - scarlet, primrose, royal blue and white - it is not an understated cap, or one to greet a player who has imbibed too well on tour. Most of Manderston's players are from the farming community and the gaudy cap seems incongruous amid the firm handshakes and steady gazes of the brawny lads. Very useful if a batsman is checking the outfielders and it's dark; the equivalent to a miner's safety lamp.

Lying between Berwick and Duns, Manderston is one of those village clubs dependent on the patronage of the Big House. The estate workers at Manderston House laid out the ground under the guidance of its owner, Sir James Millar and the first

game was played in 1899. Sir James loved his sport; he owned two Derby winners, and he took the view that the estate workers needed healthy exercise at least once a week. 'Mens sana in corpore sans', as they say in Duns. After the estate diminished between the wars, anyone from the locality could play for Manderston and today, some travel fifty miles from Newcastle or Edinburgh to play in the beautiful five-acre grounds. Surrounded mainly by conifers, with the stunning backdrop of Manderston House, the ground is on an incline but the square is level. The club only play about five games away from home - hardly surprising considering their location - and once a year they go as far north as Cupar (eighty miles) and south to

Blagdon Park (sixty miles). Passports are not needed, even though the youngsters may be told they are!

They play only friendlies, preferring fun rather than the grim pursuit of league points. In such an under-populated area, it is sometimes difficult to raise eleven players for their one team. The farmers seem busier than ever, while the need for young blood has never been more keen. Yet there are indoor nets in the winter and the club goes out of its way to encourage boys to have some coaching. At least a couple of lads between thirteen and fourteen get a game every weekend, the only way the club can look to the future.

Manderston House is open to the public every Thursday and Saturday, and there is often a game to watch on the Saturday. A pair of sunglasses to cope with those caps is advisable

Marchwiel

MASTER BUILDERS must pay attention to firm foundations and when one of their number turns his attention to a cricket ground, one can safely assume he will do a proper job. Sir Alfred McAlpine certainly did that on behalf of Marchwiel's cricketers in the early part of this century. Since 1911 successive generations of the famous building family have encouraged cricket to be played at Marchwiel Hall, just south of Wrexham, and now it is one of the finest private cricket grounds in Britain.

The lawn from the majestic white Georgian house leads to the ground, and a dazzling display of rhododendrons curve round to the splendid pavilion, which was built just after the Great War.

A picket fence encloses the ground and the whole quality of the setting is a tribute to the patronage of the McAlpine family and the supreme groundsmanship of Bill Pound, who has lived on the estate for more than forty years. It is the perfect setting for elegant country house cricket and one cannot quibble with John Bell, Sir Alfred's grandson when he says: 'I'm genuinely proud of our ground. It needed a spot of tender, loving care in the seventies but we've revived it and I get people from all over the world writing to praise it. As a cricket fanatic, that makes me very happy.' John Bell is also entitled to be fairly pleased at his own efforts as Marchwiel's captain over the past decade. The club reached the final of the National Village Knock-Out Cup at

Lord's on two occasions and won both times in the 1980s, sweet moments for John Bell and some consolation for missing out on county cricket when he was younger. A highly talented leg-spinner, he was approached by both Surrey and Lancashire but grandfather McAlpine told him to go out and get a job instead! John contented himself with representing Wales for ten years, then restoring Marchwiel to its former glories. Now they play in the North Wales League, the strongest in the area and always finish in the top three.

The facilities for cricket are so good at Marchwiel (pronounced Markwiel), that scores of illustrious cricketers have appeared in front of the grand old house: Sir Learie Constantine, Sir Frank Worrell, Clyde Walcott, Everton Weekes, Sir Garfield Sobers, Basil D'Olivera, Arthur Milton and Jim Parks, to name just a few. In the best traditions of country estate cricket, Marchwiel CC also put something back into the local community by staging a week-long festival every July. Teams such as the Free Foresters, Cheshire Gents and Northern Nomads come and play at the McAlpine Cricket Festival, and for the last fifty years the funds have gone to hospitals in the Wrexham area. The festival was the brainchild of Jimmie McAlpine, Sir Alfred's

son, a fast bowler good enough to play Minor Counties cricket for Denbighshire. Another of Sir Alfred's grandsons (Bobby McAlpine) has also captained Marchwiel.

Now that John Bell has inherited Marchwiel Hall and moved into the gracious house, it is a safe bet that the traditions of Marchwiel CC will endure. One can only hope that John Bell's leg-spin will continue to baffle batsmen in the shadow of the Big House.

Matfield Green

MATFIELD GREEN embodies the frustrations of playing now for a typical English village side. It is that the team plays in such a lovely village. Matfield Green is the kind of place which London commuters hunt down, the type of Kentish village where only serious money gets you a house. A few miles from Tunbridge Wells, very near to Paddock Wood for the train up to London, it is an ideal retreat for the Filofax brigade who contribute little to village life, except work for a nanny and the man who fixes Volvos. Playing for the cricket team comes low on the list of social priorities. Those who got the club going a quarter of a century ago have had to move away because prices have been forced up, and so voluntary work for the cricket team declines.

This season Matfield Green had to pull out of the Kent Village Sunday League because they could not afford the sixty pounds a week a groundsman demanded. So they just play friendlies on Saturdays and seem reconciled to losing their best players to nearby established clubs like Maidstone, Tunbridge Wells and Linton Park. It seems the way of many a village club in the 1990s. Without the dedication of Jack Wish and Frank Hudson in the mid-sixties there would not have been cricket at Matfield Green. Jack, a farmer, provided equipment to get the village green licked into shape, while Frank, the local policeman, knew enough people in the area who could be dragooned into playing. They literally started from scratch, but the main advantage was that every

player came from the village and mucked in. Eventually Matfield Green was promoted to Division One of the Sunday Village League, but came straight back down again and now they are out of it.

It is a situation viewed with sadness by Peter Tourle, one of the club's founder members: 'I was born and bred in the village and played for them while still at school. It was great fun to see everything taking shape and to be told by so many touring sides what a pleasure it was to come here. Now it's the old story, only a few want to do the work that's just as vital as turning up to play. We're short

of money and we're going through a bad patch.'

Perhaps symbolically, the duck pond beside the cricket pitch where Peter Tourle once fished is drying up. The ball is often hit into the pond but the carp which used to swim in it have been taken out as the water level fluctuates. There are four pubs within a radius of three quarters of a mile (indicative of the money sloshing around some parts of Matfield Green), and a butcher's shop and garage in the main street of the village. Just a couple of miles from the A21 road leading down to Hastings, it is the ideal spot for village cricket - but for how much longer?

Milstead

ONE OF THE GREAT advantages of trees around a cricket ground is the aesthetic one. Milstead's looks lovely, with flowering cherry trees, ashes, enormous horse chestnuts (one of them more than three hundred years old), all blending delightfully with the thatched pavilion. Such wooded density has a practical asset as well - the M2 motorway lies a quarter of a mile away, yet at the cricket there is not slightest evidence of that.

Milstead lies between Sittingbourne and Maidstone on the North Downs, deep in the heart of Kent's fruit growing belt. The population of Milstead village is two hundred and ten, and not one house has been built there since the last war. The village is one large conservation area, and the cricket ground is also in tune with that spirit. Although the club has been going since 1857, they moved to its present site, in the heart of the village, just after the last War. They paid a peppercorn rent to the owner, Mr Rex Boucher and when he died a few years back, his widow sold it to the club for ten thousand pounds. Thanks to various grants and a great deal of fund-raising work, the loan for the purchase was paid back impressively quickly, and now Milstead can look to the future with confidence. They have played in the Kent Invicta League for the past four years, chugging along in mid-table, and they run two elevens. In the words of their secretary, Brian Spicer: 'We satisfied the younger players by going into the league because that seems to be the kind of competitive cricket they like, but we rely on good *members*, rather than just good cricketers. The best clubman may not be the best cricketer and I know which one is more important to us.' Much voluntary work is needed at Milstead CC - it takes six hours with a pick-up mower to do the outfield and the wicket and pavilion are of a high standard because of the unselfish example set by several club officials. Younger members need look no further than Gil Trinder for the right attitude to village cricket. When the club moved to its present site, Gil (a relative of Tommy Trinder, the famous comedian) devoted his efforts to ensuring Milstead had a worthy club. His fund-raising efforts were legendary and as captain for twenty years, he carried the club for a long time. Now life president, Gil is delighted that the playing inheritance is being carried on by his son and grandson.

If newcomers to Milstead CC are ever in doubt what standards need to be matched to be accepted as a good clubman, the gates to the ground provide a constant reminder. A plaque beside the gates reveal that they were put up in memory of Stan Kenwood - scorer, teaboy, treasurer, secretary and player for fifty years at Milstead. Sadly, Stan was only 59 when he died, but those gates are a fitting monument to the very best kind of village cricketer.

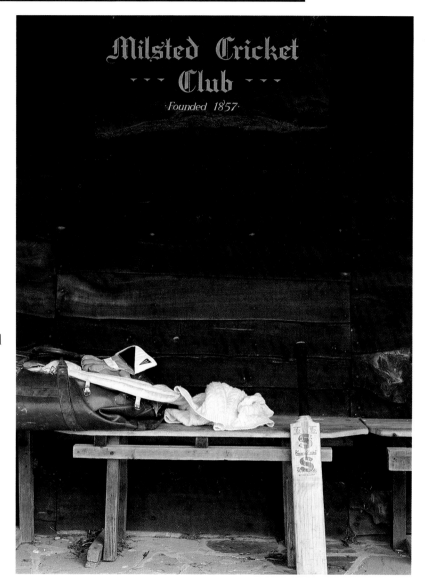

Mobberley

ONE OF CHESHIRE'S oldest churches looks down on Mobberley cricket club. Built in 1245, St Wilfred's has surveyed cricket at Church Lane for a hundred years. It has also been the home of six rectors from the Mallory family. When the club was formed in 1876, George Leigh Mallory, played for them, as did his grandson George - the mountaineer of the 1924 Everest expedition. Mobberley is now mainly a home for commuters and those engaged in farming. Many generations of farmers' sons have turned out for the club and only eleven presidents have seen service: they tend to die in harness!

With so much National Trust land surrounding the ground, it is hard to realise that the M6 thunders just two miles away. Around twenty-five thousand pounds has been spent over the past two winters on extending the ground on the north side, installing a second all-weather practice wicket, revamping the clubhouse kitchen and modernising the pavilion. Mobberley play in the Cheshire League, they run two senior sides and the junior section is thriving. The youngsters come from as far as Macclesfield (twelve miles away) to play. Their standard is sufficiently high to make some of the seniors look over their shoulders at the coming generation, especially as all the junior teams play league cricket.

Farokh Engineer's brother, Darius, played ten years

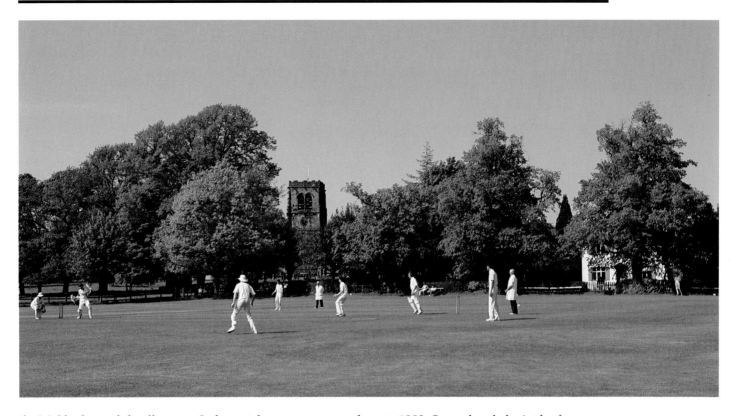

for Mobberley and the illustrious Indian wicket-keeper/batsman has regularly appeared with his customary bonhomie at the club. Brian Statham and Cyril Washbrook, those two great Lancastrians, have also played there. The politically correct will be glad to know that women's cricket is greatly encouraged at Mobberley, after Rachael Heyhoe-Flint brought a team there in 1982. Since then ladies' sides from New Zealand and Australia have stayed in the village and fought keen contests. The gospel of Mobberley cricket has spread to places such as Malaysia, Singapore, Hong Kong and Kenya over the past decade and the club's next tour is to South Africa for Christmas 1993.

Newtown Linford

LYING DEEP IN the heart of Leicestershire's fox-hunting countryside, the village of Newtown Linford is not just a hazard for foxes. If you walk down its main street, past the cricket ground, prepare to don the metaphorical tin helmet. Many a straight hit lands in the street, pings a passing bus, or bounces into the gardens across the road. This is particularly so when the county players of Leicestershire turn out in one of the many benefit games hosted by the club over the years. The professionals do tend to hit the ball a good deal further than the club players, and profuse apologies are often proffered to the neighbours.

At the other end of the ground, there is a steep slope leading up to a side of Bradgate Park: eight hundred acres of lush parkland, with deer and ancient oak trees. Bradgate Park was part of the Grey family estate and this is where Lady Jane Grey lived before she became Queen of England. Her reign lasted only nine days, but fortunately Newtown Linford CC has shown greater staying power. It was formed around 1900 and moved to its present site just after the First World War. The facilities are excellent, and the club have won the Leicestershire Club Cricket League five times since it started in 1974. There is a healthy flow of young blood, mainly due to the encouragement of their fathers, who still play. An element of continuity is even evident in their summer tour: since 1957, they have been based in mid-Wales, at Newtown.

Two items of local knowledge are important when playing here for the first time. A good hit straight back past the bowler towards Bradgate Park is not automatically a four. Many a fielder has trotted after the disappearing ball, in the mistaken belief that some kind soul will be throwing it back to him from over the boundary line. Yet the slope can be deceptive and invariably the ball holds up, tantalisingly close to the edge. There is every chance of an all-run five. Secondly, one large oak tree stands proudly inside the playing area. Until recently, the local rule was that if the ball hit the tree, it was four. There were times when visiting fieldsmen throwing the ball back from near the boundry would hit the tree by mistake and be horrified to see the umpire signal four. That has now changed; the tree is part of the ground, so keep on running if the ball hits it.

There is no doubt that Newtown Linford CC will keep on running. The club is in good hands and manages to marry the convivial with the highly competent on the field of play.

Nomansland

IT IS GIVEN TO FEW cricketers in a lifetime to have the chance of hitting the ball into the next county, but that is a definite possibility on the village green at Nomansland. The playing area is in Hampshire, but behind one of the boundaries lurks Wiltshire, a brawny drive away. Until a few years ago, the geographical permutations were even more bizarre. The Lyndhurst to Romsey road ran *through* the cricket ground, at one stage just nineteen yards from one of the wickets. So a fast bowler would usually begin his run in Wiltshire, deliver the ball to a batsman in Hampshire, and was often smashed back into Wiltshire: the bowler would have to look both ways as he launched into his run-up and the passing traffic caused

nightmares to the fielders.

The square has since been moved back, so that the road is now the boundary. There are still a few hazards on match day, though; a selection of pigs, horses, cows, sheep and donkeys pay regular calls to the green, doing very little for the over-rate. Four large beech trees and a war memorial are all inside the playing area - you can't be caught off any of the hazards and you score two runs if the ball comes back into contact. A sense of humour is essential to play at Nomansland, but ability is also preferred. The team play in the First Division of the New Forest League and they have been runners up in the past two seasons. They have thirty playing members and seem to have no difficulties

attracting teams to such an idiosyncratic ground. Since 1987 they have an impressive pavilion, opened by Nomansland's most famous son, John Sillett. After John managed Coventry City to their famous FA Cup win at Wembley in 1987, he was delighted to come back to his old village and, with the cup-winning side, play a cricket match to commemorate the opening of the new pavilion. With Coventry's goalkeeper, Steve Ogrizovic, showing just why he had played Minor Counties cricket with Shropshire, the footballers eased home by twenty runs - but not before a cameo bowling stint by John Sillett near the end. He still dines out on his 2 for 2 in one over!

Nomansland boasts about three hundred inhabitants, a pub right on the green and a post office, but its main claim to fame is that remarkable cricket ground. Just behind the green is the site where William of Rufus, King of England was accidentally killed by a hunter's arrow in the twelfth century. So far, no other tragedies have disturbed life on the green, a fitting tribute to the sharp reactions and stiff braking of thousands of car drivers since the cricket team was formed in the 1920s. An insurance claim by an injured fielder would be an interesting test case!

Outwood

NOT EVERY CRICKET CLUB can boast a foreword in its excellent centenary brochure from the then Foreign Secretary, but Outwood CC is entitled to quiet satisfaction on many levels. The brochure came out in 1987 and Sir Geoffrey Howe - local MP and an Honorary Life Vice-President of the club - did the honours, pointing out that both his wife and daughter had been keen cricketers. They would have been welcomed at Outwood, where a flourishing ladies' team has been active since 1926.

The village of nine hundred inhabitants is in a conservation area and the ground, leased from the National Trust, is a haven of tranquility. Only the occasional whine of a jumbo jet reveals that Gatwick Airport lies eight miles to the south. To find Outwood's ground, you must turn down a track opposite a windmill - and here again the timelessness of the area is accentuated. The windmill, built in 1665 is the oldest working windmill in England, open every Sunday afternoon. Hence the presence of a windmill on Outwood's club badge.

The facilities at Outwood are first-class , and since a Cricket Week was started in 1975, the club has enjoyed the company of many sports celebrities - from Bob Wilson to Jimmy Greaves to Peter Parfitt, John Snow, Fred Titmus and John and Bill Edrich. Back in the 1950s, strong links with Surrey CCC saw the likes of Peter May, Micky Stewart, Jim Laker, Tony Lock, Alec Bedser and

Ken Barrington enjoying social cricket at Outwood. Each season, Outwood hosts more than forty matches, from Kent Village League to friendlies.

Lovers of cricket literature are also indebted to Outwood CC for providing the author A.G. MacDonell with inspiration when he wrote the classic chapter on village cricket in his book, *England, Their England*. McDonell played at Outwood in 1922 and captaining the home side was Major J.R.E. Cunliffe. Now the Major was, to say the least, a colourful cove. He would arrive on horseback at the ground, then lead Outwood onto the field, wearing white gloves and sporting a monocle. He thoroughly disapproved of running while batting and dealt almost exclusively in fours and sixes. Close scrutiny of Major Hawker's character in *England, Their England* indicates that the author made some precise mental notes on Major Cunliffe of Outwood. Also playing in that game at Outwood in 1922 was a promising young actor - Ralph Richardson.

Anyone who wishes to know more about the deeds of Outwood CC need only ask Geoff Last and a veritable torrent of statistical data tumbles forth. Geoff is the one who can tell you about the day in 1966 when Kevin Norris took 6 wickets in 6 balls, as Outwood dismissed Turner's Hill for just SIX. Outwood is a highly impressive club in a glorious location. And its members seem to have struck the right balance between keen cricket and respect for what the game means. As Geoff Last wrote in the centenary brochure: 'Let us not forget that what we do today is the history and tradition of tomorrow.' Already, in its second century, the club has outlasted Sir Geoffrey Howe in public life.

Oxted

THE CRICKET SOCIETY knows a thing or two about the game in this country and when the Oxted ground was used as the colour photograph for the front of the Society's 1991 Christmas card, it was hard to fault the choice. Master Park, where Oxted play, is lined on three sides by oak trees. The fourth side is open, which is just as well since the view is wonderful - first the tower of St Mary's Church, built in 1086, and then the North Downs. Master Park was left in trust for the sporting benefit of the good folk of Oxted and today, tennis, soccer and cricket are all played there. Fortunately an avenue of oaks separates the cricket from the football pitch and the twain never meet.

Oxted is on the border of Surrey and Kent and the cricket club straddles the M25 for fixtures. They run three elevens and a burgeoning Colts section and their first team play in Division Two of the strong Surrey League. The club was founded in 1890 and its excellent centenary brochure was proudly on display at the ground when the MCC and Surrey CCC came to play there in 1990. The brochure, an essential guide to Oxted cricket, is still on sale at the club. Many a Surrey beneficiary has enjoyed a lucrative match at Oxted and players of the stature of John Edrich, Peter May, Sir Garfield Sobers, Ken Barrington, Mike Smith and Micky Stewart have graced the proceedings over the past thirty years. The connection with Surrey

goes back for as long as Oxted's playing history. Oxted can boast of a former player who went on to captain Surrey and England (H.D.G. Leveson-Gower), a fast bowler (Neville Knox) described as the best he had ever seen by his Surrey comtemporary Sir Jack Hobbs, an England batsman (Errol Holmes) who was acknowledged to be one of the most punishing players seen in English county cricket between the two wars. Tony Lock, a great slow left-arm bowler, played on Sundays for Oxted, even a week or so after he had helped England regain the Ashes in 1953. The man who demoralised Keith Miller, Lindsay Hassett and other Australians at The Oval thought nothing of turning out for Oxted that September of '53 and he was even happier when he managed to score 63 against West Kent Wanderers, to add to his expected harvest of wickets.

Even though Oxted is right in the heart of the Surrey stockbroker belt, the cricket club is not wealthy. They have to pay the management of Master Park for the use of the pitch and must rely on their own fund-raising efforts to keep going. Since the wooden pavilion was built thirty years ago, bar takings have become a fundamental source of income and the club hopes to make a profit of around one thousand pounds a year to keep facilities up to scratch. They are now deemed sufficiently good to allow Oxted to stage a few Surrey Second Eleven games a season, so the happy association with The Oval continues to prosper.

With around forty senior playing members and a satisfactory supply of young players coming from Oxted County School, the omens for Oxted's bi-centenary are entirely favourable. So long as man can play cricket in front of Norman churches like St Mary's, there will always be enthusiasm for the game.

Poplars CC

ONE NORMALLY ASSOCIATES big-hitting and the pursuit of soaring sixes with village cricket - but not with this club. When they play at home, you are out if you hit a six. That is not the only bizarre aspect of life on this particular cricket ground. One of the sightscreens is cream coloured and just happens to be the side of the local pub.

First a rendition of the obvious. They are called Poplars CC because a line of poplar trees fringe one side and embrace the pub - also called, strangely enough, the Poplars. The cricket area used to be an orchard attached to the pub and all praise to the brewery, Wadworths, for resisting the temptation to turn it into a carpark and chase the profit motive. Perhaps Wadworths had the good sense to realise that cricketers playing next door to one of their pubs in a quiet corner of Wiltshire would eventually mean thirsty cricketers in the evening.

The 'six and out' rule stems from an awareness that passing traffic through the village of Wingfield meant regular hazards from cricket balls flying out of what is a very small ground. Any batsman with the ability to time the ball could get sixes with defensive shots, and it is very rare to see an all-run two on this ground. A single or four is the staple scoring diet, so the batsmen have to steel themselves to play the ball along the ground in the approved coaching manner. The problem is that Poplars CC is proud to be known as a pub side, declining to play in leagues because they do not take the game that seriously, and blissfully aware that a comfortable girth is almost compulsory when you represent the honour of your local pub. All those ingredients (plus the odd pre-match pint or three) tend to induce in a batsman the desire to send the ball soaring away into the wild blue yonder. Often the scorer has to ink in the doleful dismissal 'out - hit ball for six' in his ledger, as bucolic habits die hard.

Situated on the Wiltshire/Somerset border, the village of Wingfield houses only about a hundred souls and its cricket team plays in a fifteen mile radius of Bath. Batting adjustments for away matches have to be made, and sixes are then recorded, but they have been managing the transition happily enough for the past twenty-five years. They are - shall we say - a mature side and tend to delay their entrance in the season until late May, when the square has dried out and the poor drainage on the ground has been put to the test. Then the side is off and running, playing around forty friendlies a season, including midweek games in front of the Poplars pub. Afterwards the splendid Wadworth's 6X gets the proper treatment. They give a whole new dimension to beer matches.

Pott Shrigley

THEY CALL THEMSELVES 'the Hill Men' at Pott Shrigley, apt testimony to the Derbyshire Hills that circle the ground of this pretty Cheshire village. The Peak Park starts at Pott Shrigley, continuing over to Matlock and the Peak District, and with Derbyshire just eight miles a way it is ideal hiking territory. Just behind the pavilion lurks the Nab, a wooded area beloved of hikers, and an ideal vantage point to watch the cricket.

The club was formed in 1919, after the young men of the village had returned from the War, determined to enjoy one of the traditional features of English rural life. The ground belongs to the parish council and its foresight means the provision of trees many years ago has paid off: it is now handsomely lined with trees. It appears a smallish ground - indeed last year the first team scored 200 and lost five times - yet officials point out it is the same size as Macclesfield town's ground, where Minor Counties cricket is played. Until 1976, water for teas had to be ferried from St Christopher's Church, but since then, showers and an electricity supply allow the club to compete on level terms in the Cheshire League, both on and off the field.

With around forty juniors at the club, taking part in three leagues, officials have taken steps to ensure the best players do not all grow old together at the same time. There is another spin-off from running such a vigorous youth policy: fathers bringing their sons to Pott Shrigley find their enthusiasm has been rekindled, and the odd Sunday game becomes a full season. Pott Shrigley prides itself on its family traditions: the president, Mrs Lilian Tute, sits out in all weathers, supporting her two sons, while the two offspring of the chairman, Mike Hart, are regular players. The doyen of the club, Fred Wridgley - associated with Pott Shrigley since 1949 - also keeps a keen eye on his son's progress. As Derek Brown, the club secretary says: 'We had to progress. If we hadn't gone for the juniors twenty years ago, we wouldn't have survived. We now have four with the NCA Coaching Certificate who help the young players along, and the benefits are obvious. Cricket clubs die these days without youngsters.'

The next stage in the club's development is an artificial wicket, and a new roof on the pavilion. They have been lucky enough to pick up a grant of four thousand pounds towards that, courtesy of the Foundation of Sport and Art, a charitable organisation set up in 1991 at the initiative of the Prime Minister. Pott Shrigley is not the only club grateful that John Major is a cricket fan!

Saltaire

SIR LEARIE CONSTANTINE, that great man of West Indian cricket, once described Saltaire's ground as one of the three prettiest he had seen. It is in a park, with elm and ash trees a welcome accompaniment and the River Aire running along one side, with a long pole on hand to fish the ball out. Many fine deeds and cricketers have been seen here since the club started in 1869.

The village of Saltaire (five miles from Bradford) was founded by Sir Titus Salt in the middle of the nineteenth century. Sir Titus was in the precise mould of those Victorian entrepreneurs whose exploits used to bring a tremor to the voice of Mrs Thatcher. After discovering the breed of Alpaca Goat in Argentina, he returned to Yorkshire and set up a mill to profit from the distinctive wool. Soon he had hit on the idea of a model village and after the factory there followed a school, a hospital, houses for the workers and Roberts Park for their recreation. Thus Saltaire was created, a model village for a model entrepreneur. No alcohol anywhere in the village - Sir Titus was a staunch Quaker - and even today no beer is consumed on Saltaire's ground.

Sydney Barnes was one of the greatest bowlers of all time. After taking 189 wickets for England in just 27 Test Matches, he decided to make a lot of money from his abilities, by playing in the leagues, rather than for a county. He played for Saltaire for eight seasons, taking a staggering 904 wickets at an average of just 5, and today he is still acknowledged to be the greatest player ever to perform in the Bradford League. Barnes, like any other man keen on business, knew the coffers at Saltaire CC were overflowing on his behalf, so he negotiated some princely contracts for himself. In the 1922 and '23 seasons, Barnes was pulling in almost nineteen pounds a match, plus talent money and a benefit match each year. In his last few seasons he was paid two pounds extra for coaching sessions and he also pulled in travelling and removal expenses. At today's prices, nineteen pounds a match cannot be far short of one thousand pounds. Barnes was worth it as far as Saltaire was concerned.

Another great England bowler played for Saltaire: Jim Laker went to the local school and turned out for the club when he was sixteen. His all-round talents eventually attracted Surrey and the rest is history. In fact anything to do with Saltaire's cricket history seems to be within the memory of Alf Burgoyne. Alf was the club's secretary for fifty years and at the age of ninety-two, he can still recall the great days of Barnes and Laker. Jeff Driver, the first team captain, has had the good sense to place Alf Burgoyne's reminiscences on tape and one day there will be a comprehensive history of this fine Yorkshire club.

Sedgewick

THERE IS A BOARD on the wall of Sedgewick cricket club's pavilion which neatly sums up the yawning gulf between the aspirations of the ordinary village player and that of an England cricketer. When Graeme Fowler came up to the Lake District to play in a benefit game, he was interested in the board detailing every hundred made at the Sedgewick ground since this century. He noticed the highest score of 150 and announced calmly: 'I'll beat that today.' He did, making 166. That sort of self-confidence makes an impression on village cricketers.

Three miles south of Kendal, Sedgewick is a very pleasant place to play cricket. A traditional English pavilion, green and white in colour, affords a

rewarding view of the fells. There are hills and trees as far as the eye can see and the occasional visit onto the pitch of a deer adds to the rural charm. Sedgewick is now a retirement village - the nearest pub is three miles away - but the cricket ground is in excellent condition. The square is laid in the established way, with cinders below the top soil; it is one of the best batting surfaces in the local league. It is carefully tended by two young players, Carlton Mason and Dale Martindale.

The ground is dominated by a splendid large house owned (until recently) by the Wakefield family for generations. It is now being converted into luxury flats. The club was formed in 1864, for the benefit of workers at Sedgewick House and those from the

Gunpowder Works, a mile away - now a caravan site. In the mid 1960s, the club folded. Too many players had moved away from the village and not enough voluntary work was being put in on the ground and the pavilion. When it was re-formed in 1976, the club officials decided that any office holder had to live within three miles of Sedgewick House and now the unsung army of volunteers have helped revive the fortunes. The first team play in the premier section of the South Lakeland League, after working its way through all five divisions, and the second team turns out in the League's fourth division. There is also an Under-sixteen and an Under-twelve side, and a Family Eleven for those who like undemanding cricket on a midweek evening. The family connection is strong at Sedgewick: the Willacy brothers are the sons of a doyen of the club (Robin), while Nick and Jason Dalzell are carrying on their family tradition.

There is also a thriving ladies' committee at the club, formed three years ago to boost funds. A series of barbecues, car boot sales and jumble sales have helped Sedgewick to stay in the black, a considerable achievement when there is no clubhouse bar. The rebuilding scheme launched in 1976 seems to have put down substantial roots.

Sheepscombe

MEMO TO ANYONE planning to visit this gem in the North Cotswolds - take a camera, a healthy hunger and check your exhaust isn't loose. You meet at the Butcher's Arms in the village, the focal point of the community and the place where all the club's crucial decisions are made. Savour the pub's relaxed, jukebox-free ambience, its splendid real ales and massive ploughman's lunches. Just after two o'clock the convoy departs and after negotiating countless twists and turns, the summit is reached - sometimes with a trailing exhaust pipe. The view is worth the tortuous journey. Two things instantly assail the senses - the stunning backdrop of the Painswick Valley and the stillness. It is so quiet that those in the middle can hear every conversation from the pavilion, so beware disparaging remarks about the umpiring.

The shape of the ground is idiosyncratic. Watching from the pavilion is like spectating on top of the world, as the slope filters down to the square. At the top end, it dips away alarmingly: batting from the pavilion end, you can only see the bowler's head if his run-up is more than ten yards away and a good memory for fielding positions is vital. Long-on and long-off cannot be seen and the fielding captain has to bellow the location of the ball as it soars into the outfield. If the ball beats the wicket-keeper, four byes are a certainty. At the other end, only two batsmen since the war have cleared the pavilion with a six.

Umpire Fred Hunt - a farmer of seventy-five summers - is splendidly dismissive of the need to be in the right position to judge a run-out and relaxed in his assessment of the number of balls left in the over. On occasions, Fred turns out as player, sporting the buckskin pads once worn by the great Walter Hammond fifty years earlier. Any questions about Hammond normally elicit from Fred a two-pint answer. Stan Beard, a comparative stripling of forty-three years at the club, looks lovingly after the square. It is now a fine batting wicket, improved by mains water at last in the pavilion. No longer do the players have to stagger up the hill, gear in one hand and water buckets in the other.

Sheepscombe Cricket Ground is a setting to test a poet's descriptive powers. How appropriate that it should be owned by the poet and novelist, Laurie Lee, who hails from the village of Slad, just two miles across the valley. The man who ...*Walked Out One Midsummer Morning* and drank *Cider With Rosie* bought the ground in 1959 and leases it to the club for nothing.

Shipton-under-Wychwood

WITH A NAME LIKE THAT, the village just had to have a cricket team and it has - a good one too. On the Burford side of Shipton, the ground is opposite Shipton Court; it is surrounded by trees, including a long avenue of lime trees down one side. An old wooden pavilion - with bar - has rendered noble service since Shipton first played there in the 1930s, and the sophisticated equipment at the club's disposal is impressive, considering there are only about two thousand people in the area from which to find players and money.

They run two teams and play in the strong Cherwell League. In recent seasons they have made some progress in the National Village Knock-Out Competition, but secretary Mike Meredith is worried that the players are all growing old together: 'We used to have a youth team but there are no schoolmasters at the club now to look out for young players at school and bring them along to the club for coaching. At the moment we are all right for players, but you've got to look to the future.' Shipton do keep an eye on their neighbouring village of Milton-under-Wychwood, to see if they have any promising youngsters, but they point out with some relish that Milton play in an inferior league and the village rivalry only extends to relaxed friendlies. Hard to imagine a local derby full of fast bowlers shouting 'oh, jolly good shot, my friend!' or batsmen nodding 'well bowled' as they survey the ruins of their stumps, but Shipton seem to feel Milton deserve encouragement.

A few of Shipton's players live in the village, others in nearby Witney, while a couple come from Swindon, thirty miles away. Another, Ken Withers, occasionally jets in from some foreign clime to play. Ken is a film cameraman who disappears to the other side of the world several times a season on some mysterious assignment, then returns with a few tall stories. He is also nearing seventy years of age, but still bowls canny medium pace for the Second Eleven. The wags in the side often suggest Ken should film his own bowling action, just to see how low his arm is these days, but he has the laugh on them, turning out at the pipe and slippers age. Must be the country air around this lovely spot in the foothills of the Cotswolds. One thing is certain; Ken's cinematic talents will be required by the club should the day ever dawn when Shipton reach the Cup Final at Lord's.

Shobrooke Park

THE CANADA GEESE that fly over this lovely ground at six o'clock every night have a perfect view of a vintage village cricket scene. You can almost set your watch by them. All the ingredients for sublime village cricket are here at Shobrooke Park. Wonderful thatched pavilion, a line of small lakes over the boundary's edge, set in glorious countryside between Exmoor and Dartmoor. Sometimes they even have Devon cream teas during the match: Shobrooke is a typical Devon village of about three hundred folk, not reliant on the tourist industry. The area is studded with marvellously evocative Devonian villages: Upton Hellions, Stockleigh Pomeroy, Newton St Cyres and Brampford Speke.

Shobrooke Park is owned by the Shelley family, local landowners, and the club has played there for just over a hundred years. Now it plays in the Devon League, the only way to keep the young cricketers interested - otherwise they would end up with clubs perceived to be more ambitious. So the best youngsters are in the first team while the average age of the Second Eleven is around forty-five, full of old romantics who can now appreciate the symmetry of the Canada geese formation and what a pleasure it is to be playing on such a ground.

Many old hands recall one particular day as the most perfect of their careers. North Molton came down from Exmoor for a match that ended in a tight finish. So tight that North Molton's scorer was convinced that his side had won by one run while Shobrooke's scorer adamantly maintained they had won by one wicket. The matter was resolved in the proper, civilised manner, with both sets of players repairing to the Red Lion, a quarter of a mile away, leaving the scorers to their obduracy. To this day, both sets of club records state a different result to that match.

Shobrooke's senior players are certain that they have had the slowest bowler in their ranks that cricket has ever seen. Robin Coaker has more or less retired now after years of bamboozling batsmen who would seek in vain for the ball as it was propelled high into the air. Some swear the ball had ice on it when it returned to the business area and Robin's team-mates would titter as the batsman would have about six thrashes at the ball on its way down. One day, Somerset CCC came to play in a benefit game and they played one I.V.A. Richards in the side. Now Viv was then the most destructive batsman in the world and he was determined to take up the challenge. Unbelievably he had Viv caught at mid-on, off the third swipe to the same delivery, and although the great man took it gracefully, it was clear that he was bemused

at bowling that was distinctly un-Caribbean. Instead of smell-the-leather, Viv had time to polish-the-leather. Yet the dismissal is in the book and no one can ever take it away from Robin Coaker as he begins every second conversation with the dreaded words: 'Did I ever tell you about the time I got Viv Richards out?' Robin probably does not share the opinion, but he has been even luckier than that in his cricket career - he has been able to play at Shobrooke Park.

Sicklinghall

SICKLINGHALL IS one of the many unsung, unheralded clubs in Yorkshire that keeps battling on, enjoying the occasional successes and relishing the environment in which it plays its home games. Even though the ground is just about a hundred yards from the Wetherby-to-Harrogate road, it is a tranquil haven. The array of sycamore, beech and oak trees around the ground help keep modern cacophonies at bay and the white fence girdling the square-shaped pitch gives an air of neatness. The ground is at Stockeld Park, a mile out of the village of Sicklinghall. The club has spent a happy last thirty years there after moving from the village, and the players are working hard at improving facilities. They hope to reach an agreement with the owners to allow them to build showers and larger dressing-rooms and the club is in the process of spending fifteen hundred pounds over three years to improve the quality of the square. They cannot afford a groundsman so they muck in themselves. They seem to be making encouraging progress.

The club, formed in the 1920s, plays in the Wetherby and District League. The first team is back in the First Division after a triumphant promotional season in 1991; they were getting bored with early finishes, supping the first pint at the Scott's Arms at 6.30 and now they are facing sterner competition. They have a hard core of about twenty-six playing members, plus around fifteen juniors. The juniors also play in Leagues, to familiarise them with the necessary disciplines when they graduate to adult cricket. With the market town of Wetherby three miles away and posh Harrogate eight miles in the other direction, there is no lack of competition among local cricket clubs. Sicklinghall know that few players from other clubs will join them because their facilities are just basic, but they can deal with that. More and more sides in the Wetherby League seem to feel that the way to success is by importing West Indian or Australian players, with money stuffed in the back pocket, but that would never be the way for Sicklinghall, for two reasons - they lack the finances and facilities, but more importantly they feel that it is not the right way to play village cricket in Yorkshire.

There is one way to be sure of getting a game with Sicklinghall - if your name is Wood. At the moment John Wood, his brother Dave and John's four sons - Andy, Steve, Martin and Phil - all play for the club, an age span from twenty to forty-eight. Not forgetting John Wood's brother-in-law, Dave Barwell. Five of the Wood cricketers live in the same house at Sicklinghall, and their female companions remain unimpressed at the constant cricket talk. No point in complaining about it to grandfather, though: old Jim used to play for the club, and still watches the boys in all weathers. Jim's dad was the first to play for Sicklinghall, starting the Wood dynasty. All of them pretty good players, which kicks any whispers of nepotism into touch. One of these days the Woods will be able to put out an entire eleven - but will any of the ladies offer to umpire?

Southborough

THIS IS THE IDEAL SPOT for anyone grappling with the A26 on the way down to the South Coast. You will come across a cricket ground between Tonbridge and Tunbridge Wells and there is plenty of room to pull over. Southborough cricket club cheerfully claim they were on that road first, long before the motor car, and passing car-drivers simply have to take their chance with a flying cricket ball. Hard to argue with that - the first match on Southborough Common was played in 1794 - and cricket on the green is an integral part of life in Southborough. All the necessary ingredients are there for relishing a lovely Kentish cricketing day. The Hand and Sceptre pub right on the green, two large oak trees inside the playing area (four if the ball hits the trees, if it's thrown back through the leaves, just keep running between the wickets), the reassuring chime of St Peter's Church and a mound on one side of the green that gives an unrivalled view down to Tunbridge Wells. With proper respect for the traditional order of things, the umpires are guided by the chimes of St Peter's, even if the hands on the clock tell a different story: when it chimes five o'clock, it is time for tea.

Southborough play on the common, courtesy of the parish council and the locals are unashamedly traditionalist. They describe Tunbridge Wells (founded in 1604) as a new town and they are sticklers for good behaviour on the cricket field.

One visiting player was banned from ever playing again at Southborough after some histrionic behaviour and a home player who threw his bat into the pavilion after being dismissed was made to write a letter of apology and pin it up on the pavilion wall. Colin Young, the club chairman says: 'Good companionship is one of the most vital elements of all cricket, there must be no ifs or buts about bad behaviour. We bring on the youngsters as cricketers but also as well-behaved sportsmen, because that is just as important.' Colin kept wicket at Tonbridge School to the leg-spin of the precocious Colin Cowdrey and they have remained firm friends in the intervening years. Colin Young's love affair with Southborough began in 1940 when he was still at school. He has masses of local newspaper cuttings, old posters advertising matches at Southborough going back to 1828, and he is full of salty tales of cricket on the Common. There was the time in 1821 when the Gentlemen of Maidstone came to play for money and after the Gentlemen of Southborough lost to them, they removed the wheels of the opposition coach. In response the Maidstone players threw rocks at their hosts! Five years later, the local ladies played the Ladies of Tunbridge Wells for the prize of four

bottles of gin and three bottles of gunpowder tea.

There are fifty-eight cricket clubs within a ten-mile radius of Southborough but they are pretty successful in the upper echelons of village cricket. They have won the Kent Invicta League and been runners-up in recent years, and with two Second Elevens, the chance is there for young players to be imbued with the correct attitudes to the game. Every Wednesday night, around fifty local youngsters receive instruction from three qualified coaches, and they play league games on a Sunday morning. Lucky lads. One hopes most of them appreciate men like Colin Young and cricket havens like Southborough Common.

Stanway

A VISIT TO STANWAY in the Cotswolds is essential for those who treasure fond memories of the salad days of village cricket, when no one played in a league and the sun shone every match day. Although the pavilion has been re-thatched in recent years, there is no sign that the harsh realities of this decade have imposed themselves on the ground. An afternoon at Stanway cricket club is the perfect antidote to the stresses of the modern world.

The ground is right beside the small road leading from Stanway to Stanton, south of Broadway and the Vale of Evesham, and the wooded slopes of the Cotswold escarpment form a stunning backdrop. The outfield is a real test for the newcomer, with evidence of the 'ridge and furrow' system of medieval farming. Out in the deep, the undulations are a hazard for the unwary. Local legend has it that Stanway breed cricketers with one leg shorter than the other, so that they can patrol the boundaries, and it is certainly no area to place any of the more statuesque of your fielders!

Stanway House looms through the trees, hundred and fifty yards behind the pavilion. One of the most beautiful Jacobean manor houses in the Cotswolds, it was one of those places where the great and the good gathered particularly during the 1920s. Among them were E.V. Lucas, John Galsworthy, A.P. Herbert, G.K. Chesterton, H.G. Wells and

Walter de la Mare, a few of whom were also avid cricket fans. None more so that the man who persuaded the owners to let him take over the house for a month in midsummer - J.M. Barrie. More than thirty years before his first visit to Stanway House, the creator of Peter Pan had formed his own wandering cricket club, 'the Allahakbarries' (a word coined from the Arabic for 'God help us!'), and as soon as he had settled into his love affair with Stanway, he turned his attention to the cricket ground. He brought sides there to play the village team and one day he remarked that if he could only take a hat-trick, he would build the club a new pavilion. The local cricketers knew a soft touch when they met one and despite Barrie's modest attainments as a bowler, the hat-trick was contrived. The result is one of the glories of Cotswold cricket. The pavilion is set on staddle stones, built entirely of wood, faced with rustic cladding and crowned with thatch. It has been re-thatched twice since the 1920s, the last time at a cost of ten thousand pounds - a considerable fund-raising achievement by such a small club.

Stanway cricket club has not only attracted the 'literati' but also some famous cricketers. In 1933, an England eleven played a Gloucestershire Select and such notables as Herbert Sutcliffe, Morris Leyland, the Nawab of Pataudi, G.O. Allen, R.E.S. Wyatt, Tom Goddard, Charlie Parker, Charlie Barnett and Walter Hammond boosted the funds of a local charity. The scorebook of that match is in the proud possession of the club. The club entered the Cotswold Hills League recently with some misgivings, but it would take a good deal more than scrapping for points on a Saturday to tarnish the golden memories of genuine village cricket at Stanway.

Swan Green

I F YOU HAPPEN to be tootling in your car along the A35, Southampton-to-Bournemouth road, sharpen up your reactions when you near Lyndhurst. Five miles outside that busy holiday resort some serious action takes place beside the A35 at Swan Green cricket club - and passing cars have been known to take the brunt of a well-struck ball. Club officials are well aware that if a ball hits a car, or goes through the windscreen, they are liable. As yet they have not needed to pay out on personal injuries, but insurance premiums were up to three hundred pounds for the 1992 season to give cover of a million pounds.

The ground is bang in the middle of the New Forest, an area of Hampshire that has eight million visitors in an average summer. In July and August, when hordes of Japanese and American tourists tumble out of their coaches to take photos of this quaint version of baseball, the risk from a flying cricket ball is that much greater. Horses and cows do get hit occasionally, but their pain threshold seems to be higher than that of the average human.

They are used to coping with money worries at Swan Green CC. It is an expensive area to live in, so many of the local players have had to move away, but they still come back for the cricket and to help raise funds. In the past year, they have had a big push to renovate the pavilion and they made it with the aid of jumble sales, a log run on Easter

Sunday and subscriptions. With thirty players in the club, an annual turnover of twelve hundred pounds giving a profit of three hundred and fifty pounds is no mean achievement.

With two oak trees on the outfield, the stream that runs all the way round operating as the boundary line, and the Swan pub on the green, it is no surprise that the setting is a magnet for those who do not know their off-break from their off-drive, but know what constitutes a genuine slice of little old England. After hundred and twelve years, there seems no earthly reason why Swan Green CC should not continue to be a visual delight and a challenge to insurance salesmen.

Ullenwood

THERE ARE SOME stunning little cricket grounds in the North Cotswolds, an underrated area, replete with nature reserves, country parks and bracing fresh air. Such a one is at Ullenwood, a mile or so from the village of Birdlip. The ground is set in a hollow and the view from Crickley Hill - one in six, it is steep - is enchanting. There are trees all around, mostly beech and chestnut, and the area marks the start of the Cotswolds Hills, running on to Slad, through Birdlip and Cranham. After a brisk walk up to the country park, those of an archaeological bent can explore an Iron Age Fort - or simply look down on the cricket.

With both Gloucester and Cheltenham eight miles away, that pleasant Gloucestershire burr is much in evidence. One local rule invariably affords consternation to the first-time visitor. A large oak tree stands about fifteen yards inside the boundary. If the ball hits the tree, the umpire must call 'dead ball' and award three runs. So the languid fielder pursuing the ball up the slope entreats it to make contact with the oak tree, thereby saving his side one run and himself a chase. Hard luck on the batsman who makes contact and thinks 'that's four' as it soars away in the deep mid-wicket or extra cover region, but that is the beauty of local rules. A notice in the clubhouse informs the players of the rule but does not prepare them for the particular umpiring signal -

both arms are outstretched, elbows and hands are bent and shaped together in the outline of a tree and the call of 'three runs' echoes around the hollow. One newcomer who smashed a ball over mid-wicket and saw it smack high against the oak tree was mortified to be denied the three extra runs the stroke deserved.

The wicket is flat and true, testimony to the hard work of Terry Dernie and John Chandler, two stalwarts at the club for many years. The slope on either side of the square does lead to some interesting chases uphill after the ball; in such circumstances, young lads can be very useful in key fielding positions! Slip is definitely the place for the more solid senior citizens of the team, with so many treacherous undulations in the outfield.

A friendly, warm club with its own clubhouse bar, Ullenwood would rather play friendlies all the time, but they have to play on a Saturday in the Stroud Building Society League, just to get some fixtures. Sundays are given over to friendlies. Six touring sides come to Ullenwood every year and promptly book in again for next season. Definitely a fixture for those of a photographic leaning - and for those sadists who enjoy watching older players lumber up a slope after a ball that eventually passes them on the way down!

Warborough and Shillingford

THEY SEEM TO HAVE got everything right at this club. The village green is tucked away in a secluded corner of Warborough village, between Oxford and Henley-on-Thames. The thirteenth-century church of St Laurence is just behind the pitch which is surrounded on three sides by elegant houses and neat cottages. To the east there is a panoramic view of the Chilterns. To the right of the pavilion, the splendid Six Bells pub sells the excellent local Brakspear's Ale. The supportive hosts, Jim and Rosemary Bridge, chalk up forthcoming fixtures on the blackboard beside the dish of the day.

The pavilion, dating back to the 1890s, is perfectly serviceable, with showers and electricity and the pervading atmosphere on Warborough Green is one of enjoyment that cricket is still thriving there. There has been cricket on Warborough Green since the 1790s and until the hay rights were bought out by the club from the parish council thirty years ago, the ground had to be cropped before any cricket could be played. On the

pavilion, a plaque commemorates the sterling efforts of the Rev. Herbert White, vicar of Warborough for more than forty years in the mid-nineteenth century and a true benefactor. He paid for some almshouses out of his own stipend and established a primary school in the village, again out of his own pocket.

To its eternal credit the club does not play league or knock-out cricket, even though they have many fine players in the ranks. They have a large membership, and at least three fathers are currently playing alongside their sons with justifiable pride, but the club has always resisted having to scrap for points in a league. They run a Saturday side and two Sunday sides and somehow manage their difficult task of giving everyone the chance to bat or bowl, while ensuring the match does not drift into uncompetitive waters. They play the best type of village cricket on Warborough Green, sporting yet competitive, relaxed yet traditional. It is a haven for touring sides from all parts of the country and there is often a midweek game. The club is rightly proud of its juniors' section and they play in cup and league competitions to harden them up for adult cricket. In 1987 they managed a clean sweep of Oxfordshire trophies in all three age groups under

the wise tutelage of John Hill and Roger Pickering.

Around nine hundred people live in Warborough and Shillingford but on some days there have been up to four thousand on the green to see the star players of Somerset over the past decade. The club established a happy relationship with Somerset CCC and Peter Denning, Viv Richards, Joel Garner, Vic Marks and Peter Roebuck have all brought sides up to Warborough for a benefit game. Not even the mighty Ian Botham or Viv Richards managed to win the Manor House Challenge in any of those benefit games. Tim Martin, a vice-president of the club, lives in the elegant Manor House, on the south of the green and he has happily carried on the tradition of paying out five guineas to the batsman who breaks one of the Manor House windows. That is a fairly long hit, but not outside the range of Botham or Richards, but so far the only man to get near is a Dutchman with a touring side in the 1970s. He hit the front door third bounce.

So if you happen to wander down to Warborough Green one day and see a succession of batsmen aiming for the lofted six, do not automatically assume they are aiming for an early tilt at the Brakspear's. Not many prizes these days are measured in guineas.

Warkworth Castle

WHEN OFFICIALS OF cricket clubs aver that 'there's a lot of history attached to our club', they sometimes overdose on hyperbole. Not so Warkworth Castle in Northumberland. The ground and its environment positively reek of antiquity. Within two hundred yards of the field, the ruins of a splendid castle stand sentinel. It was there that the first Earl of Northumberland and his son Harry Hotspur laid plans to unseat Henry IV from the throne of England. Harry Hotspur had been born eight miles away at Alnwick Castle - he was called Hotspur because he was so active it seemed his spurs were always on fire - and when he was killed at the Battle of Shrewsbury, his father was given the news at Warkworth. He then set out on his fatal mission to avenge his son's death, leaving William Shakespeare to immortalise the story in *Henry IV, Parts 1 & 2.*

So Warkworth Castle is a bull target to those combing the Northumberland coast for local culture. Cricket afficianados are rather keen on the ground as well. Under the guidance of Tommy Hogg, the cricketing doyen of the area, the club has been flourishing for a number of years. They won the Northumberland League in 1991, and players travel from as far as Newcastle, thirty miles away - and who can blame them? Warkworth Castle has reached the quarter-finals of the Village Knock-Out Trophy on two occasions, and no one should bet against an appearance one day in the final at Lord's.

They may be a fair way from city life, but the players of Warkworth Castle are not star-struck country lads. In 1975, Bob Willis and Rohan Kanhai came up to play in the club's centenary match, and the former England captain returned for another game in 1981, his benefit year, bringing a Warwickshire Eleven. Willis has been back again since to play, and he recalls days spent at Warkworth Castle with fondness: 'Very, very hospitable. Many don't know I'm a North-Easterner, born in Sunderland, and I love that rugged, open countryside near Warkworth. My liver took a severe bashing at that club. Tommy Hogg doesn't take no for an answer when he's at the bar!'

So for those playing at Warkworth Castle for the first time, have a big breakfast before setting out - and pack an extra roll of film for your camera.

West Fairleigh

A GROUND WITH A VIEW, this one in the centre of Kent. From the pavilion, you can look out over the Medway, with the village of Teston snuggling below, just half a mile away. On a clear day, you can see... not quite for ever, but a very long way. This village four miles from Maidstone is one of those that seems to have kept the urban sprawl at bay very successfully. At the last count, only two hundred and fifty-seven people lived in West Fairleigh (pronounced 'Farley'), and there are just one street, one pub and no shops at all. There is a strong agricultural and market garden flavour to the area and in midsummer the hop-picking brings a few more to the village, but otherwise life meanders along very pleasantly down in West Fairleigh.

A mature oak tree stands inside the boundary, its roots spreading nearer and nearer to the square; four runs and dead ball if the tree is hit. There are many beech and oak trees in the four acres of cricket ground and the thatched pavilion blends in pleasantly with the surroundings. The gales of 1987 severely damaged the pavilion and it cost six thousand five hundred pounds to refurbish. The club cannot play at home on Sundays. The local farmer has an agreement that the Sabbath shall be honoured and the parishioners at All Saints' Church - which overlooks the ground - are happy with that arrangement. So, in the words of Micky Back, the club doyen: 'Some play for other clubs on a Sunday, while others like me, take orders from our wives.' Not that Micky misses out on his cricket. He expects to play around five games a week in summer around the Maidstone area for any club that contacts him, but he readily admits his heart is with West Fairleigh. 'I've been player, groundsman and general dogsbody here since 1962, and we are a good, friendly village club. I wish we could get more young players, but there you are. There's no school nearby and although the village has a football club, none of them seem to want to play cricket. So we're all over thirty-five in the cricket club. But we keep going, have a lot of laughs and play some good cricket without needing to travel very far.'

For such a small club, West Fairleigh have a good recent record. They won the Kent Invicta League in 1981, have been runners-up twice since then and they have a respectable record in the evening league and the knock-out competitions. They run just one Saturday team. The club was formed in 1920, nine years after the football side that plays elsewhere in the village. Although there are few houses in the village, West Fairleigh is comparatively large - probably because it was hit by a plague in the Middle Ages and survivors built away from the centre of the village. And yes, there is an East Fairleigh and the

cricketers drink there at the Bull.

Not an area that encourages the property developers, West Fairleigh - but one that encapsulates the ageless charm of the traditional summer game in the perfect ambience.

Wighill Park

THERE ARE MORE than one thousand cricket grounds in Yorkshire, but surely none with such short boundaries as Wighill Park, near Tadcaster. Lord Hawke, captain of Yorkshire during their halcyon period early this century, had many redeeming features, but modesty was not one of them. He owned the ground at Wighill Park and after his playing days with Yorkshire ended he continued turning out on his home pitch. As he got older and slowed up, he decided he wanted to protect his batting average, so he decreed that the boundaries must be shortened. Since then, fours, sixes and singles have been the norm Park and little in between. A total of around 230 is now the nearest thing to security for the batting side in

45-over-games at Wighill Park. A year or so ago, one of their bowlers was the unfortunate recipient of six sixes in an over against Eskrik Park.

It would be hyperbolic to state that a compass and ordnance survey map are essential to find the ground, but you do have to concentrate on the directions. It lies a mile and a half from the village of Wighill, six miles east of the market town of Wetherby, and it involves an unmade track, two fences (don't forget to close them, the farmer gets annoyed), and a cattle grid. There are trees to each side, a farm behind the pavilion, and a fence all round to keep out the sheep. A newish pavilion does not have a bar, the White Swan in Wighill does the honours, one of the many fine pubs in an area close to the brewery town of Tadcaster. The ground really is in the middle of nowhere and that is part of its attraction. With the nearest road more than a mile away, the absence of motor car sounds is a blessed relief.

Wighill Park are in the fourth division of the Wetherby League and they play cup games and the odd friendly on Sundays. They run two teams, both in the league, and although they have forty-seven players registered, they do lose some to other clubs with better facilities in the area. Unusually for Yorkshiremen, they do not treat the game of cricket with undue seriousness. Their secretary, Tim Barton says: 'We're just a good set of lads who like an enjoyable, competitive game, but it ends there. We like a laugh and we're nowhere near as po-faced as some clubs around here. Four of us come from Leeds to play, and that's a forty-mile round trip, but we wouldn't dream of playing anywhere else.'

Wisborough Green

LOCATION MANAGERS for television series are notoriously hard to please. But when the BBC comedy series *Ever Decreasing Circles* needed a typical village green to stage a cricket match they found the perfect place - Wisborough Green. So the 'luvvies' came down to West Sussex with their clipboards, gaffers, clapperboards and boom mikes and the deed was done, with the estimable Richard Briers playing the role of bumbling nitwit to perfection. Wisborough Green cricket club provided most of the players, the BBC made a satisfactory contribution to funds and the locals were able to appreciate how much time goes into recording something that passes on screen in the blink of an eye

One can see why Wisborough Green caught the eye, though. It is surrounded by roads and cottages, with one pub (the Cricketers) on the green and another (the Three Crowns) equally adjacent. In the interests of fairness, the players frequent both pubs in equal measure after taking the edge off their post-match thirst in the club bar. Phil Collins, the rock star, drinks in the Cricketers (he lives at nearby Loxwood) and Mike Rutherford, lead guitarist in Collins's group, Genesis, lives at Wisborough Green. Both are vice-presidents of the club, they happily attended the annual dinner and are judged to be all-round good eggs who are granted their privacy when necessary. Phil and Mike play every year in a charity match on the Green for a team called the Wilting Willows and the autograph-hunters are attended to with good grace.

They have played cricket for around hundred and fifty years at Wisborough Green and now they run two senior elevens and a Colts side. A year or two back, club officials worried about the decline in young players took the initiative and wrote to other local clubs, suggesting a Colts' league to get the youngsters interested. There are now eleven sides in the league, they play 25-overs matches on Sunday mornings and then watch the seniors in the afternoon. From such planning spring the good adult players of tomorrow.

The square is small and cars going past often take the impact of a good hit. The club is insured for such damage if it comes to it, although those who stop and watch are deemed to be willing to accept responsibility. The doyen of the club, Laurie Cheesman (now the groundsman) recalls the days when a slim young Indian came and played occasionally for them. The Nawab of Pataudi used to visit his guardian in the village when he was at Winchester College and one day, he managed to sneak into their Second Eleven. He scored 74 and after that, a place in the First Eleven was his for the

asking! A few years later, the Nawab lost an eye in a car accident and a brilliant career at Test level seemed over. But he fought his way back up the ladder and when he made a brilliant 100 against England at Leeds in 1967, the good folk of the village could happily lay aside their patriotic feelings and cheer the brave prince.

A thriving club in the Sussex Invitation League, Wisborough Green goes from stength to strength. And they don't even have to touch Phil Collins for a contribution to club funds!

Chapter 3

VILLAGE CRICKET IN ACTION

'GOD GAVE US MEMORY so we could have roses in December' wrote J.M. Barrie and although the creator of Peter Pan was the ulitmate cricket romanticist even the most hardened cynic can see what he meant. One sweetly driven six can make a summer for the dedicated coarse cricketer. It warms him throughout the winter, even when the club's averages are handed out at the annual dinner and he has to justify retention of his place with a batting average of two, one catch (and that an involuntary one) and a total of three overs of bowling described by his waggish team-mates as 'buffet bowling' - help yourself. Come the spring, that six over the trundler's head in late June has assumed significant proportions: 'I can still do it,

just a matter of getting fit.' Do not mock the coarse cricketer. Just like leg-spinners, beer with an original gravity of more than 1040, and London taxi drivers who read the *Guardian*, they are worth preserving.

One day every player will arrive at the village green with his own cricket case, a bat that set him back the normal weekly wage, spare trousers for fielding and for batting, tablets to aid dehydration during a long innings and a computer print-out of the team's current averages. Make no mistake, that breed is rapidly spreading. Such desiccated calculating machines belong in serious club cricket, where every match is played for points, a 'winning draw' is something deemed preferable to a 'losing

demon fast bowler's end. Verily, the law of Sod dogs him every faltering step of the way, but he comes back for more the following week, despite the following disillusionments...

THE CAPTAIN - He is the one who makes a show of extreme reluctance when offered the job in the winter. He runs through the litany of excuses - nagging wife, growing family, work commitments - but his brow blackens when it appears the committee has taken note of his objections. After a show of wrestling with his conscience that usually only comes with a RADA scholarship, he allows himself to be talked back into the post. A few months later, he learns the first cruel lesson of captaincy - everyone wants to bat at number six and bowl first change. Only the useless volunteer to take responsibility.

The captain needs to be imaginative - to claim the credit if the team wins and blame the fates otherwise. It helps if he has a memory for names, rather than a tactical memory. The burly fast bowler with menacing ways is not impressed by a call of 'a little wider at third man, Jason' when he is emphatically a Bill. Whenever he suspects the opposition is weak, he puts them in ('to make a game of it lads, the pubs

draw', where the captain allows a maximum of six players to dominate batting and bowling, where the youngest son is deputed to video father's on-drive from the boundary's edge. Their definition of a 'character' is someone who buys drinks for the opposition and appears to enjoy their company. The coarse cricketer, on the other hand, views the vagaries of the game with the stoicism of an Ethiopian refugee. For him, the shower always runs cold, the bar is out of peanuts and he is run out by the side's best batsman trying to get away from the don't open round here till seven'), and at tea, the score is 250 for 2, with a declaration a remote possibility. The captain gratefully takes the proffered new ball, then remembers he has no bowler with even the rudiments of swing bowling at his disposal. Within four overs the shine is disappearing because the ball keeps rebounding from a stone wall on the mid-wicket boundary. It is then lost in the undergrowth, the replacement one is tonked all over the district for the next two hours and then the original ball is mysteriously discovered at tea-time by one of the local (salaried) urchins. It then proceeds to swing in the gathering gloom as if Wasim Akram were playing for the opposition. Your skipper's field-placing owes much to intensive research of Alf Gover's *Book of Cricket Tactics* rather than an awareness of cricket on the village green. So the opposition play the mow and the dab to untenanted areas of the pitch while extra cover and cover point do not field a ball throughout their innings. They do become very adept at catching the ball as it is thrown back by a strolling yokel. The presence of a left-handed batsman is usually the cue for chaos, leading to three leg-slips and five men in the covers, all because the leader has forgotten to shout 'left-hander!'

The captain is usually a poor judge of a youngster's abilities. He puts all his faith in his tyro, only to see his slow bowling savaged. The feckless wimp then misses an easy catch, he rubs the affected part of his soft hand with touching misery and his captain feels sorry for him, putting his arm around his shoulder consolingly. An hour or two later, the pimply youth reminds you that he needs a lift home now to get to that rock concert and that he has forgotten to bring any tea money. In contrast, the opposition adolescent walks in to bat, looking as if a good cry is imminent. You wonder if he is the product of a broken home, the victim of a social worker's misguided idealism and if his diet is all that it should be. Two overs later, he has unfurled a series of glorious off-drives and you are cursing his coach.

When it comes to setting an example, the captain is usually found wanting. He may be the one with an honours degree, the one who can tell you the England batting order at Old Trafford in 1953 and how to spot the googly, but he turns out to be the player who tries to square cut a yorker, with just four to win, six overs in hand and your best batsman stranded at the other end. On the village green, cricket omniscience never walks with practical skills.

The inexperienced village green captain is as vulnerable as those bright-eyed subalterns at Ypres. He will have entered the campaign determined to uphold the standards of decency and fair play, with trebles and crisps all round in the bar afterwards, but soon he comes up against the *realpolitik* of the game. Within a month, his own personal nadir is reached. They lose to a team of unpleasant yuppies who ponce around in the field, performing 'High Fives' like Curtley Ambrose clones, appeal for

everything, apply retrospective legislation ('Didn't I tell you, old boy? It's twenty overs after seven o'clock, not six thirty'), and then your last man is out in the final over as the pavilion lights shine out and you need a miner's safety lamp to get back to sanctuary. In the club house, their captain knots his cravat, puts down his mobile phone, claps you on the shoulder, asks 'What's your poison, squire?', buys you a half, then asks you for a contribution to their centenary appeal. At that moment, the charms of a prolonged Sunday lunch, meandering through the papers and a desultory spot of weeding in the garden appear irresistible. Even more when your Youth Policy starts bleating about his lift home.

NEWCOMERS - A problem. You cannot rely on them to tell the truth. The player who drops out on the morning of the match tells you 'Don't worry, I've got a guy who's a much better player than me, he's got a Blue'. He fails to tell you that the Blue was for hockey. Nor does he mention that the late replacement lives fifty miles in the opposite direction and that he is banned from driving. When you meet, he says, 'Of course, I haven't played for years' but you still back a hunch, put him up the order and his words are chillingly accurate. He looks as if he has never batted since the days of a Labour Government yet he is not good enough to get a touch to a series of unplayable deliveries. He hangs around at the crease far too long, your best hitter does not even get to the crease and at tea-time, he returns to the pavilion, creased in smiles, delighted at his unbeaten ten in eighty minutes. A few overs into their innings, he sidles up and says, 'I did tell you that I have to leave at six thirty, didn't I? The party's been arranged for absolutely yonks.' So the player who lives nearest to the late replacement also has to leave early, the opposition do not offer two substitute fielders and you are thrashed by eight wickets.

One example of the Law of Sod in this area: the one who pulls out on the morning of the match is not only your best player, but he has the team kit. And beware of the ambitious late replacement who enjoys the day too much and nurses dreams of a takeover. In the bar, he says diffidently, 'I'd love the odd game if I could be fitted in, I've just moved into the area.' That cold gleam in his eyes is attributed to shyness, but within a year he is captain. Soon his friends from the Chianti circuit are being drafted in. The roller is used between innings, sight screens are placed at both ends and woe betide the village

elder who stands beside one of the sight screens as one of the new men is batting. Having been brought up on good wickets at their minor public schools, they can bat; they shout 'Waiting!' rather than 'No!' when negotiating for a quick single. Within a year the takeover by the village commuters is complete and the bucolic element fades away to form a bowls club. And yet you rarely see any of the new brigade's wives doing anything as menial as preparing the teas.

PREPARATION - On match day, this takes the form of counting to eleven and then heaving a huge sigh of relief. Anything more ambitious than that is a waste of time. Those zealots who feel the need for a knock-up on the outfield must realise that you are then playing your best strokes at 2.20, rather than 4.30 when it is more advisable. The major preparation should be of a bacchanalian nature. Where is the nearest pub? Is it in the Good Beer Guide? Can the tactical team talk be held in the pub garden without the distractions of slides for children and hungry labradors sniffing at our ploughmen's? Can you get a curry nearby, three hours after the game has ended and you have drunk back the fixture? Is there a phone box, for the purveying of feeble excuses to the seat of domestic power?

After the local ales have been supped and the previous day's county cricket discussed, attention is turned to the forthcoming entertainment. The ritual of the pitch inspection is enacted. The team gather around the wicket - the ones who have at some stage scored a fifty call it 'the track', and it is advisable to walk up and down the twenty-two yards, offering little other than prolonged staring, the occasional pressing of the finger and a sporadic 'hmm ...'. Usually you will only know it is the match wicket because two sets of stumps will be placed at either end, so it is better to appear wise, rather than open your mouth with a forecast about its qualities that will end all speculation about your wisdom. Finally, the tension is broken by the senior player - 'it'll do a bit' he opines and with that his opinion is taken up with all the alacrity of Henry VIII's courtiers. Nobody quizzes him about what that phrase actually means, but they have all heard it on Test Match Special at some stage. That leaves the captain with a problem; his opening batsmen do not wish to take first innings (because 'it'll do a bit'), while his opening bowlers have now left the scene and are recycling their lunchtime beer behind an oak tree. Wisely surmising that his fast bowlers may well have supped unwisely yet well, the captain opts for the wisest decision - he hopes to lose the toss and have his mind made up for him. His indecision is final. Showing the sort of hard-nosed sagacity that brought him leadership, he calculates that he has a fifty per cent chance of avoiding responsibility. He strides back to the pavilion, hoping he looks confident.

EQUIPMENT - The opposition fielder with the rather fetching sweater is assumed to be a top batsman because he does not bowl or indeed rarely touches the ball. He looks impressive, though, and all attempts at quick singles in his direction are spurned. Only afterwards do you discover he is wearing a tennis sweater and was roped in at the last minute. Compare the scruffy oik who turns up in a mauve shell-suit, changes into greyish-white gear, squash socks and khaki pads, then uses his bat like a scythe and never misses once with his only shot, the slog over mid-wicket. Your main batting hope saunters out to the crease with pristine white pads, a sweat-band on each wrist, and ironed shirt collar turned up in the approved manner. He is bowled by a grubber before a red mark can appear in

the middle of his expensive new bat, with the fashionable scoop on the back and the extra rubbers on the handle.

Midway through the season, after the first win has finally been recorded, a groundswell of opinion positively demands a club sweater and tie. The club secretary ascertains he can get a good deal provided he orders a minimum of four dozen. Three months later his car boot is overflowing with ties and sweaters because the players who wanted them have left the club.

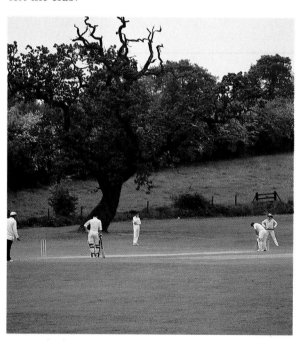

UMPIRES - The opposition's twelfth man. Stone deaf when one of his players knocks the cover off the ball and declines to walk, he possesses the sharp reflexes of a western gunslinger when one of his bowlers appeals. The following exchange is true:-

'Howzat, Dad?'

'That's out, son!'

Such an umpire rarely manages to count to six at the right time. He allows seven balls an over when your side is defending a small total and gives you a five ball over when you are on a run chase in the gloaming. Partial umpiring takes many forms of subtlety. Once an umpire ruled 'not out' when one of his batsmen was struck on the right knee in front of his stumps. When that bowler enquired the reason he was told 'too high'. Next ball, he hit the batsman on the boot, again right in front of the stumps. 'Not out' again. Why not? 'Too low'. Such arbitrators must have been weaned on the standards reached by one of the umpires in A.G. MacDonell's classic novel, *England, Their England*, which includes a glorious account of a coarse cricket match. After the opposition's best batsman had blasted his way to 52 out of 69 for 5 in no time at all, he made the fatal mistake of being hit on the chest. 'Out!' shrieked the umpire before anyone appealed. He had a keen sense of his responsibilities to his village side after umpiring for them over the previous thirty-two years with sublime disregard for the game's ethos. A few minutes before his prompt decision, he had shown the stuff of quick-witted heroism. After the said batsman had deposited the first three deliveries of the rate collector's over into a hayfield, the saloon bar of the Three Horseshoes and then the squire's trout stream, the umpire followed his conscience, called 'Over!' with three balls to go and marched promptly to square leg. In one instant, he had averted carnage to his side and guaranteed a favourable response to his fiscal failings from a grateful rate collector. Times were hard for the umpire and the rates kept rising.

For most umpires on the village green, the lbw rule remains an incomprehensible piece of legislation to all but a few bar bores. It is hard to accept the 'rub of the green' argument when you have been cheated out for your fourth successive nought and their star batsman escapes a plumb lbw on three and gets a hundred. Sometimes one of the opposition players has donned the white coat and has to make the decision and that is often made according to how well he has bowled or batted in that game - or if he has been sawn-off at the knees by someone in desperate need of a guide dog. The uncomplaining soul who stands out there for over an hour and then rushes back to pad up, only to be told about the declaration just as he is ready to walk out to bat is not a man to be ignored. Vengeance is in his gift the following week, when the insensitive captain is asking for a guard. The cute ones contrive to be on the phone or answering nature's call when umpiring volunteers are being sought, so that the captain invariably has to go out there and do the job himself. No sane cricketer wants to umpire - they never bowl that rubbish at you when you are batting, you are weighed down with sweaters when the sun is cracking the flagpole and you cannot get near one when a cage of brass monkeys agree it is a trifle chilly.

THE SCORER - A breed apart. A lifetime spent as a trade union official or traffic warden would appear to be the best training for this exercise in bloody-mindedness. When the batsman returns, convinced he was unlucky to be given out, he is told, 'Look in the scorebook' before his ire has eased. A cynical assessment of the umpire's honesty, eyesight and numeracy seems an essential tool of the trade - 'When did we agree to seven ball overs?' Timing

the enquiry from the scorebox is an art form. The bowler must be almost into his delivery stride before being interrupted by the strident cry 'Bowler's name!' If more than six balls in the over are delivered at his batsmen, he automatically logs them as no-balls, assuming the umpire had forgotten to signal. This custom mysteriously disappears when the opposition batsmen go out after tea. Watch out for the sneaky run added to the total if two of his players cross when a skied catch is taken. That is another practice that lapses after the tea-ladies have been thanked. Unfortunately for students of the duplicitous, the experienced scorer is becoming a rarity. The counter-attractions of the garden, the DIY centre, satellite television or even double time for Sunday work are luring them away. Often the job is done by a surly member of the batting side who is already out, or one of the players' girlfriends who displays the concentration of a stunned butterfly as she boogies under her Walkman.

FIELDING - When your side is in the field, the ball will always skid through a cowpat or leap off a pothole, endangering your front teeth. The one with the softest hands proceeds to pull up the ladder on the chance at the last instant, leaving it to a more athletic team-mate to dive forward in vain. After returning from the stratosphere with ice on it, the ball hits one of the hapless fielders on the head, it is then hurled at the stumps in frustration just as the captain shouts 'No!' and it speeds away for four overthrows. That rarity - seven runs off one ball - is thus accomplished with some ease.

On a personal level, you know when you have become a liability in the field once the youngest player in the side runs alongside you, expecting the ball to be lobbed to him so he can shell it back to the wicket-keeper. Newcomers to the team always say they field in the covers, that they like to run around a bit; they then proceed to give an excellent impersonation of Lot's wife after turning round. Newcomers never volunteer to field at slip to the fast bowler or the leg-spinner.

The rare, blinding slip catch taken by one of your players sees the back of their last man, a noted rabbit, when you are cruising to a 75-run victory long before opening time. When their best batsman lobs up a dolly and starts to make his way back to the pavilion in disgust, it is spilled by your team's graphic artist or pianist. He then proceeds to make a career best and buys a jug of celebratory beer in the bar afterwards. The graphic artist or pianist drops the jug.

BATTING - There are just too many ways of getting out when your team is batting. Bat and pad never seem to develop a meaningful, intimate relationship when you go out to the middle. If you take middle and leg guard, you lose your off stump, while middle and off guard sees your leg stump pinging out of the ground. Stand a foot outside the crease and you are yorked, a foot inside and you knock down your stumps attempting something

spectacular. Raise your backlift and you're bowled. Change your grip on the bat handle and it flies away in the direction of square leg.

The opposition slogger always comes off against you, turning the game in a couple of overs as your fielders scatter like missionaries to the Victorian Empire. He grins bashfully after the first couple of ludicrous escapes then, after half an hour of mayhem, he is acknowledging his fifty and confessing it is the first of his career. By July, your team is fed up with congratulating opposition sloggers on career bests.

BOWLING - Beefy youngsters who think they are quick bowlers, running in from thirty yards yet purveying medium pace tosh - mostly down the legside - play for your team. Slim, bespectacled youths who sidle in from ten yards from behind the umpire can usually transform an old ball into a spitting cobra with a flick of the wrist and an unerring ability to hit the crater on a good length. They play for the opposition.

TEA-TIME - The electricity goes off at 4.55. The ravenous labrador has eaten the sausage rolls. Younger players who sneer at the club's equipment demur when the raffle book goes round in aid of funds. On the away ground, you finally get lucky with the raffle, only to find that the prize is a free raffle ticket and another chance to try your luck. Non-smokers always win the fags and life members of CAMRA the six-can pack of Australian lager fizz.

DRINKING BACK THE FIXTURE - After coming a comfortable second, you troop off to a crouching ovation from the three members of the opposition with pretensions to sportsmanship. The others are too busy using all the hot water up before your lot can get in the showers. The captain mentions a few drinks and you perk up. The memory is still fond of the pre-match session in the nearby Dog With Eight Paws, a pleasing hostelry with six different real ales, a garden and a nice line in hot food on a Sunday. You are suddenly informed that the home team has fallen out with that particular landlord and then ushered to their new favourite. Two miles down a winding track, and a broken wing mirror later, you enter a grimy boozer with a loud jukebox specialising in rap music. The only available food is poppadams, the children have to sit in the car and there is frogspawn at the bottom of your glass of old and nasty. The opposition that bother to turn up go straight into a selection meeting, then gather round the fruit machine for some intellectual cut-and-thrust. The only conversation to be had with them is brief. When offered a drink, they pause agonisingly, examine their half-emply pint glass and reply, 'I'll just have a pint.'

It is at that moment you remember you asked your wife to pick you up at the Dog With Eight Paws. Suddenly it feels like it has been a long day.

Chapter 4

THE STORY OF THE VILLAGE CRICKET CHAMPIONSHIP

ROTHMANS, IN SPONSORING the National Village Cricket Championship for 1992 - its twenty-first season - ensure that this most popular event will continue its remarkable life of good humour, good manners, good fun stretching from Cornwall to Inverness, from Dyfed to East Anglia and Kent. But how did it start?

At a meeting in the committee room at Lord's, that 'holy of holies', Aidan Crawley the chairman of the National Cricket Association, looked out of the window and wistfully remarked that he had always wanted to see village cricketers play at Lord's. There was laughter among the ranks of the others present. But one man took it seriously. Ben Brocklehurst, former captain of Somerset, consulted Harry Constantine, now the General Manager of *The Cricketer*. Why not organise a village cricket championship with a final played at Lord's? After all, he had started the National Club Knock-Out, which had been a resounding success. Why not do the same for the grass roots of the game?

The first ally is one's wife, and Belinda Brocklehurst has never in her life shirked any challenge. Together with their *chef d'equipe*, the ever-constant Harry Constantine, they formed a plan of campaign. They agreed that what constituted a village was 'having a population of not more than twenty-five hundred people', later adding that it should be a 'rural

competitions would provide the starting point of the inter-group and thereafter the national competition. The format has stood the test of time.

The organisers have always kept the original dream to the forefront of their philosophy, cajoling, caressing, wheedling, encouraging, and sometimes, of course slapping the wayward wrist. Mind you, the Rules and Conditions of the competion state under Rule 13 that: 'The decision of the organisers on all matters affecting the competition, whether included in these rules or not, is final and binding.' And so it should be, for the greatest strength of the competition is the character and commitment of *The Cricketer* to village cricket.

Among the Rules and Conditions, those that have caused a few misunderstandings are those covered by eligibility. It is thought by many that each side should be drawn from the village itself. This is impossible to legislate, for many of those born in the village can no longer afford to live there. Even so, Burton Agnes in East Yorkshire reported in 1975 with due pride 'Our team is made up of all our own lads in a population of six hundred.' With equal pride, Bishopstone, Wiltshire, reported 'Some members live as far as twenty miles away. They willingly play twice a week and would

community surrounded on all sides by open country'. After much thought they wrote to the village clubs they knew personally. Then, armed with an AA book they wrote to some two thousand additional villages. They publicised it in their magazine, *The Cricketer,* and had an immediate response from over a thousand villages. Great enthusiasm and support came from the first-class counties. By the end of the 1971 cricket season seven hundred and ninety-five clubs had been accepted and were divided into thirty-two groups whose local knock-out not hear of playing for any other team.' The rules state that a player must have played at least eight games for the club within the previous three years and first-class cricketers are barred from the competition until they have reached the age of sixty.

One apologetic president telephoned to say that, in his absence, their captain had played a young lad (who had scored 78 out of the side's total of around 120) who was a 'ringer'. The club had made matters worse by referring to the player by one name in the scorebook, another on the field and yet another in the bar afterwards. But the most telling of all was the letter received from a club secretary after a query about the qualifications of one of his players. 'He has played for us on every Sunday since he was fourteen. For four years before that he was our official scorer, and for four years before that he was the boy who put the numbers up on the telegraph. If you want to go further back than that, and I am now writing not as club secretary but as the father of the boy concerned, I can assure you that he was conceived in the pavilion.'

Rothmans (UK) Limited's first involvment was way back in the early 1960s when they sponsored the International Cavaliers. In 1992 they took over the sponsorship of the National Village Cricket Championship, in its twenty-first year.

The final at Lord's in August is now one of the most firmly established events in the cricketing calendar, with an atmosphere unlike any other game at headquarters: family fun coupled with a high standard of cricket.

Cricket can still be played for sheer enjoyment and this is the over-riding message of the competition. Any village side entering the Championship and expecting to win needs its head examined. To do so it has to win nine games all over the country in vastly differing conditions from the end of April to the beginning of September, before the final. You need luck, coupled with humour and humility. You make friends out of strangers and find parts of the country you never knew existed. It is not about what one played for, or even how you played the game. It is the memory *of those one played with.*

1972 On September 9, 1972, Troon from Cornwall won the first final of the Haig Village Cricket Championship at Lord's when they defeated Astwood Bank from the Worcester-Warwick border by 7 wickets in 33.4 overs. After a delay due to heavy overnight rain, Astwood Bank

were put in to bat by Troon's captain Terry Carter. Astwood Bank's captain, John Yoxall, who had opened the season with an undefeated 138 in an early round, played confidently partnered by John Robinson. But in the 17th over he was bowled and his captain followed immediately. The score read 69 for 2. Brian Spittle and Rob Taylor rebuilt the innings to good effect adding 70 for the third wicket. Spittle and Davies were out in consecutive overs. Troon's Peter Johns came back on to bowl from the pavilion end. Astwood Bank lost 5 wickets in 6 overs for 9 runs, and the left arm of Johns returned the impressive figures of 5 for 27. Astwood Bank finished their 40 overs at 165 for 8.

Only 23 came from Troon's first 12 overs, but Brian Carter started matters moving, 50 coming in 16 overs. If his brother had started the machine, Terry Carter put it into overdrive. The twenty-one year-old, left-handed Tommy Edwards matched him drive for drive before he was lbw to Robinson for 45. Carter reached his 50 in forty-two minutes, was dropped, and in the 34th over hit Robinson for 4 and 6 to win the game. A fine end to the game. His score of 79 not out was not bettered in the finals until 1988, when Kevin Iles hit 91 at Beckenham.

The competition got off to a good start and produced some phenomenal performances. Aston Rowant (Oxon) scored 304 for 4 in their 40 overs against Dorchester on Thames. Temple Cloud (Somerset) managed 303 for 5 against Dulverton who were bundled out for 49. In the following round Temple Cloud scored 264 for 6, bowled Merriott out for 45, and went on to lose to Evercreech. J. Bobbin of Mulbarton & Swardeston (Norfolk) produced the bowling performance which has only been bettered three times in the twenty years of the competition. In the permitted 9 overs Bobbin took 9 Great Witchington wickets for 1 run.

1973 Troon won the title for the second year, defeating Gowerton from South Wales by 12 runs in failing light. Troon had set Gowerton 176 to win, and eighteen-year-old Adrian Daniel hit 3 offside boundaries that crashed into the fence outside the

Tavern in the 2nd over. He slowed down a bit after that but reached his 50 with a hook for 6 in the 20th over.

Winning the toss Troon were made to struggle for runs, not least by Gowerton's groundsman, Bill Thomas. He bowled from the Nursery End, spectacles glinting, in half-mast cream. The trousers were constantly hitched higher as he walked purposefully back to his mark. Shirtsleeves

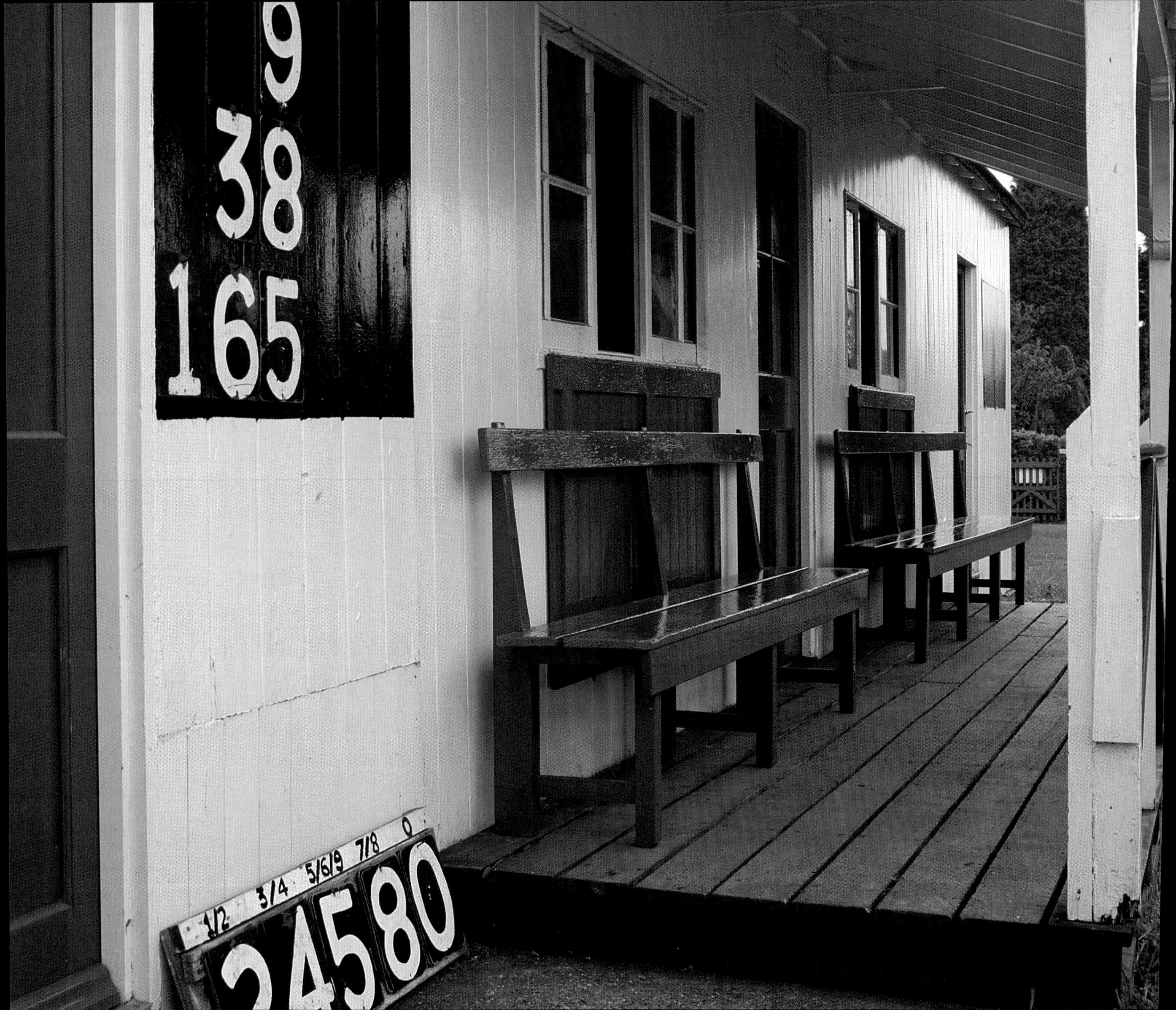
9
38
165
1/2 3/4 5/6/9 7/8 0
24580

buttoned at the wrist and a green sun shade as used by newspaper editors completed the effect of a 'great character'. His seemingly innocuous left-arm delivery, not dissimilar to that used by troops in the trenches lobbing hand-grenades, with masses of loop, deceived Terry Carter. Brother Brian took his place and in batting through the final 26 overs to remain undefeated at 70, set a defendable total and won the Man of the Match award.

1974   Substantial cash and whisky prizes were offered by Haig - the latter particularly appreciated since the season started and ended cold and wet.

The final at Lord's was washed out. The game was played, thanks to Warwickshire CCC at Edgbaston the following Sunday. In spite of heavy showers, Bomarsund Welfare of Northumberland defeated Collingham of Notts by three wickets. Set to make 110 to win, the Northumbrians lost their first wicket to the first ball of their innings. Howard Hailey played the anchor role and batted for one and a half hours for an undefeated 44 in the 38th over. He was duly awarded the *Daily Mirror* 'Man of the Match' by Ben Brocklehurst and made the best and shortest of speeches, saying, 'I got the Man of the Match, but there were eleven men of the match'.

1975   The glorious summer enabled the Haig championship to be completed without a hitch. It saw the triumph and departure of Gowerton, whose population had exceeded the arbitrary two thousand five hundred and therefore made them ineligible. Their opponents in the final, Isleham of Cambridgeshire, could not have been more different. All the players lived within two miles of their village green.

Isleham won the toss and nervously batted first. Run-outs played their part, as did Bill Thomas, who had exchanged his 1973 eyeshade for a fawn coloured jockey cap. Isleham totalled 120 and Gowerton passed that score in the 29th over with 6 wickets in hand.

In the fine weather Trevor Botting of Balcombe batted and bowled to considerable effect. He hit 141 against Withyham. The next round he hit 128 and followed it up by taking the first 7 Netherfield wickets for 15 runs. In the twenty years of the competition this is still the unsurpassed and unmatched all-round performance. In these two innings he hit 19 sixes and 24 fours - 210 in boundaries out of his 269 runs.

1976   Eight hundred and thirty-four villages

entered the competition for this year. The groupings had been slightly changed, partly to conform to the new county boundaries and partly in accordance with the geographical spread of entrants.

On the day of the final, experience triumphed over nerves. Six of the Troon side had appeared at Lord's where for Sessay - the first, but not the last Yorkshire side to appear in a final - this was not only their first appearance at Lord's but also their first visit to London. Troon were put in to bat and bowled out for 113, a vital 14 runs coming off the last 2 overs. Sessay, too, had a bad start.

But after 20 overs they had struggled to 43. In the next 10 overs they lost the match, scoring but 18 runs for the loss of 5 wickets. Brian Moyle, the only spinner used in the whole match turned his off-breaks slowly and took 4 for 24. At 81 for 9 the Yorkshiremen staged a cheerful, if rustic, last wicket stand of 14. They were defeated by 19 runs.

1977 Records started to fall in the first rounds of the sixth season. In April, Ian Enters of Alfriston in Sussex equalled the Haig record for a bowler by taking 9 for 14 in his 9 overs. His figures were not bettered until 1990. But an even more dramatic piece of bowling took place at St Bees in

Cumberland. At 70 for 6 the home side needed just three runs to win off the last over. D. Cowperthwaite took wickets with his first, third, fourth and fifth balls to win the game by two runs.

No batsman had scored 200 until May 15, 1977, when Trevor Botting of Balcombe and Tim Cannon of Cokenach made 206 and 203 not out respectively. Cannon hit 13 sixes and 17 fours in a total of 287 for 3. On the other hand, Botting hit no fewer than 20 sixes in his innings, believed to be a world record in any cricket. Five of these came in one over, and he reached each of the four landmarks, 50, 100, 150 and 200 with a 6.

The two new finalists, Cookley and Lindal Moor had had fairly easy passages. The sun shone and with the short Lord's boundary it looked likely to be a high-scoring day. As it turned out Cookley, who had been put in, lost their last 7 wickets for 37 runs to total 138. Lindal Moor lost their first 7 wickets for 69 runs and Cookley ran out worthy winners by 28 runs.

1978 This could have been a disastrous year for the village competition. There was no sponsor, although *The Cricketer* was determined to keep the competition going. On top of all this the season started with four consecutive wet Sundays. After leading his side to victory at Lord's the previous year, the Cookley captain Mick Hopkins set a competition record, scoring 214 in 39 overs, incuding 5 sixes and 27 fours, whilst of the bowlers S. Brown of Rushton (Northants) took 8 wickets in 41 balls and conceded a single run.

Rain, rain and more rain enveloped the later stages. Collingham and Isleham travelled some six hundred abortive miles between the two villages. Collingham finally won a 20-over evening match with a brilliant catch of a potentially match winning hit of the last ball of the game.

At least the weather was set fair for the final between Linton Park (Kent) and Toft (Cheshire). Put in to bat, Toft were made to struggle for runs on the fastest wicket they had seen all summer. Stimpson and some fierce hooking and pulling by

Mullholland (36) added 64 for the 2nd wicket. But they took their time, Stimpson using up 34 overs for his 41. Nigel Thirkell took three wickets, and, backed up by astute field-placing and athletic fielders, constricted Toft to 130 for 8 off their 40 overs. Linton Park were given a good start by Bowles and Brattle, but Nigel Thirkell, in the later stages assisted by his brother Tim, scored an undefeated 51 to give Kent their only championship win in the twenty years of the competition.

1979 *The Cricketer* found in Samuel Whitbread & Co Ltd new sponsors who would add much to the competition over the next six years. After the first season's sponsorship Whitbread wrote: 'No one who was at Lord's on August 25, 1979 could have doubted that village cricket was flourishing under Whitbread's sponsorship. The President of the MCC, Charles Palmer, said to me in amazement, 'But the crowd is singing already and it's only the second over!' So after a memorable final the Yorkshire team from East Bierley beat Ynysygerwn by 92 runs - and still the Welshmen sang on! Each side was encouraged by the presence of a former England captain from their own county; Sir Leonard Hutton supported East Bierley, while Tony Lewis encouraged Ynysygerwn.

1980 The new decade heralded an invasion of the Welsh; St Fagan's and Marchwiel won four of the five remaining years of the Whitbread trophy. But a constant succession of wet Sundays from June to the end of August caused many headaches.

Canon Frome set a new championship record by maintaining a run-rate of $10^{1}/_{2}$ an over when they scored 419 for 6 against the luckless newcomers, Much Marcle. 16 sixes and 49 fours scattered the spectators. No one made 100, but Maurice Emburey followed his 93 with 7 for 15 to bowl out Much Marcle for 54. Similar massacres were performed by Roxwell (Essex) who made 289 for 2 and dismissed Weeley for 11. Bottesford (Leicestershire) scored 285 for 4 and bowled Belford out for 9.

Denis Luff of Longparish had a more successful season than any other batsman in the history of the championship. In nine innings, five times not out, he made 625 runs for an average of 156.25, and including 3 hundreds. However, in the final at Lord's, he was lbw to a jubilant left-handed Carson, the Marchwiel opening bowler. Longparish never looked like recovering from 13 for 3 and were bowled out for 84, only just above half of the Marchwiel total of 161. Denis Heagren and his son John of Longparish were the only father and son combination to have played in a final at Lord's, and finished the Marchwiel innings when J. Newcombe was caught father bowled son.

1981 If the organisers felt that 1980 was wet, they had even more to complain about at the start of this year's championship. In Buckinghamshire, Bledlow borrowed a helicopter from the local RAF station for a blow-dry operation on their square, but they still had to play on the outfield. The captains of Canon Frome and Colwall in Worcester determined to defy the elements. They were somewhat nonplussed when the spun coin came down on its edge and remained upright in the mud on the pitch.

The 1981 final brought another Welsh win for St Fagan's. Broad Oak (West Yorkshire) lost by 22 runs.

1982 The most remarkable match of the season took place at Aston Rowant (Oxfordshire) when the visiting Oxford Downs scored 273 for 3, based on Robert Florey's 147* in which he faced no more than 105 balls while hitting 5 sixes and 17 fours. Aston Rowant, in successful desperation, went quicker; running everything and then more. In a third wicket stand of 130, N. Lambourne reached 97* in 60 balls and J. Cooper hit 88 of 64 as the home side cruised to victory with 4 overs to spare. It was the highest aggregate total of a match, and Aston Rowant's 277 for 4 remains the top score for a side batting second.

The champions, St Fagan's, played the 1974 losing finalists, Collingham in the final. St Fagan's, captained by Ricky Needham, were a good all-round side and were never in danger in any of their nine matches. In the final, Collingham were put in to bat, and scored 148 for 9, with Gareth Driscoll carrying his bat for an undefeated 63 in 40 overs. David Mason and David Painter paced it well and it was finally finished by Roger Stevens clouting 16 runs off 5 balls for the 'Welsh Wizards' to retain their title by 6 wicket with 2 overs to spare.

1983 On the first day only twenty-three out of a hundred and fifty matches were played and it was to get worse. Frocester of Gloucester reported a 10-run win by 555 to 545 over Down Hatherley. This set the organisers looking up the records until it was realised that after being rained off twice they had settled the issue with skittles.

Two of the most successful clubs provided a final worthy of their reputations. Troon had won the Cornish group eight times out of eleven, the championship three times, and one semi-final and one quarter-final. Quarndon is an attractive village straddling the hills to the north of Derby, their ground sloping gently down towards the stately Kedleston Hall. They did not enter the village competition until 1974, when they made a quick exit. But their record since then was to win the Derbyshire group eight times out of nine - progressing further to the quarter-finals. They were not a young team, but they were to hold the trophy for their centenary year of 1984.

1984   The sixth year of Whitbread's sponsorship was also their last. They had taken over the Man of the Match awards from the *Daily Mirror* and given tankards and much beer to outstanding individual performance. The teams from the group finals all received commemorative tankards and cheques for the club funds. Their hospitality before the final in their rooms in the City is legendary. The drays which transported the teams to headquarters, captured everyone's imagination. Whitbread's collaboration with *The Cricketer* was a marriage of

the village green with the village pub.

Sportsmanship and good neighbourliness prevailed. Fillongley scored 120 for 9 against 120 for 7 by Tanworth in Arden. But when the umpires carried out an audit of affairs they increased the Fillongley score by 1 run, sufficient to give them victory. The Fillongley committe had this to say: 'We came off the field knowing we had lost. We do not want to win on a technicality. We have had several good runs in this competition and we are therefore happy to concede to our good friends Tanworth whose turn it is and we wish them the best of luck in the subsequent rounds.'

In their last year Marchwiel repeated their success of 1980 by beating Hursley Park of Hampshire by 8 runs. Good innings by Darryl Wallis (38) Trefor Roberts (27) and their captain John Bell (55) put Marchwiel in position for a lucrative last 7 overs. In the event those overs only produced 29 runs for the loss of 3 wickets. Chasing 160 to win, Adrian Aymes (56) and Paul Wright (39) put together an opening partnership of 97 by the 28th over. But Arwel Morris at medium pace took 4 wickets and Park needed 15 to win off the last over. They got only 6 to lose by 8 wickets.

1985 For this year *The Cricketer* were again without a sponsor. Scottish cricket was celebrating its bicentenary, and it was fitting that Freuchie from Fife emerged as champions.

Rowledge (Surrey) were to make a great final with them. Electing to bat, they started with promise, Tony Hook and Neil Dunbar adding 41 for the 2nd wicket - the highest partnership of the day. In 26 overs they had scored 95. But there was to be no late charge. Terry Trewartha came on to bowl from the Pavilion end, and in 7.3 overs he took 4 for 24. Rowledge had lost their last 5 wickets for 26

runs. The Freuchie bowlers, nicknamed the 'Mean Machine', had bowled a tight line and length and were supported by one of the most electrifying exhibitions of fielding ever seen on the ground. They went on to win one of the greatest games in two hundred years of Scottish cricket.

1986 Norsk Hydro Fertilizers enthusiastically, imaginatively and with much generous hospitality took over the sponsorship of the Village Cricket Championship for four years. The first two rounds got off to a good start despite the weather. Jeffrey

Westgarth of Clara Vale produced the best bowling performance of the season taking 9 for 17 to bowl out Ulgham for 109. The most remarkable hitting in the history of the competition was seen in West Yorkshire. At Stones, the visitors Carlton were struggling, only 57 runs coming off the first 20 overs. 241 runs came off the last 20. G. Cooper (127*) and K. Barrett (102*) shared an undefeated partnership of 195 off 15 overs.

For the second year running the result of the final, Ynysygerwn against Forge Valley, went to the last ball of the game, with the Welsh losing by just 5 runs.

1987 Seven years after they had lost to East Bierley in the final Longparish carried off the championship, defeating Treeton Welfare by 76 runs in a final watched by some four thousand spectators in the same happy spirit of goodwill and fun that had pervaded and was evident in the Lord's Bicentenary game a week earlier.

1988 Two main records to fell this season. Overton on Dee put the competition's newcomers in to bat, 'to see what we have to chase'. 40 overs later they knew. Andy Shorter hit 221* and Steve Walker 109*. Shorter's is still the highest score in the competition, as is their undefeated partnership of 343. In round six Kevin Iles won the game against the Oxford Downs, played in appalling conditions by hitting 133 and becoming the first batsman to score 5 centuries in the competition.

The seventeenth final of the Hydro Village Cricket Championship was the longest in its history. 120.2 overs were bowled, 41 at Lord's and 79.2 at the Midland Bank Ground at Beckenham. Goatacre won from a seemingly hopeless position. Andrew Shorter and the Himley team were the first to applaud a magnificent piece of cricket.

1989 'We won the toss and elected to bat; a wise decision.' So commented the secretary of Barkisland. His club had hit the bowling of Old Sharlston for 440 for the loss of 5 wickets to establish the all-time record in the championship.

The final, under the sponsorship of *The Cricketer*, was played between Toft and Hambledon. It was rained off at Lord's with Hambledon in trouble at 72 for 5. Thefollowing day at Beckenham, Ronnie Locke, the Toft off-spinner, opened the bowling and took 3 for 11. Hambledon made just 104. The Cheshire side were made to struggle, but Adam Caro saw them to a deserved victory with a fifth wicket stand of 40 with 5 overs to spare.

1990 Kevin Iles of Goatacre first posted notice to village bowlers when he made hundreds in his first two seasons of 1981 and 1982. In 1983 he hit two more. The same year, against the Dorset champions Ellingham, he came to the wicket after 26 overs had been bowled, but still managed to reach 102* from the remaining 14. He thus joined the select band of batsmen who had scored four centuries; B. Carter (Troon), D. Luff (Longparish, R. McQueen (Aston Rowant), R. Phillips (Fillongley) and C. Yates (Rowledge). In 1988 he became the first batsman to score 5 centuries in the competition winning the replayed final with an unbeaten 91. But in 1991 he added 2 more including the innings of his life.

Iles won the toss and elected to bat.In the 23rd over, with the score at 100, enter Iles. He reached his 100 from only 39 balls in forty-five minutes. He hit 4 consecutive sixes off the luckless Shipton, and despite delays in retrieving the ball, he hardly had time to lose his concentration.

When he was caught in the deep at 123 by the former Derby County goalkeeper Colin Boulton he had hit 10 sixes and 8 fours. It was the first century scored in any final, and one of the fastest, finest and most ferocious displays of hitting ever seen at Lord's in any form of cricket. The crowd stood and cheered him all the way back to the pavilion. The Goatacre total of 267 for 5 was the highest in the final since their own 193 for 6 defeated Himley in 1988. Dunstall from Staffordshire were faced with an impossible task. They had reached 217 for 8 to lose by 50 runs.

1991 *The Cricketer* was again without a sponsor for the championship, but kept the flag flying. The title of village champions returned to the redoubtable St Fagan's who defeated the North Yorkshire village of Harome by 17 runs. They were led again by Ricky Needham. In the championship he is one of the few to have scored 4 hundreds and in 1984 he joined the select band (now six) of those who have scored a double century when he hit 201* in only 105 balls against Wenvoe, his last 150 runs coming off 61 balls.

St Fagan's owed their win in part to two of their youthful players, Kristian Bell and Jamie Sylvester. However they were never able to dictate against the wily spin of Bowes and Dowson whose combined 18 overs yielded only 43 runs and 4 wickets. At 110 for 5, the Welsh were wilting. But Williams, Mitchell and Rosser the last pair remained undefeated after a 6th wicket stand of 45 runs. Needham noticed the stranglehold the Harome spinners had imposed and soon introduced his own. The shrewd field placings of Lawlor and Hardwick were to prove so hard to get by that after 16 overs Harome had scored only 28 for 1. David Collier and Tom Marwood started to stir things up, but with 10 overs left the required scoring rate rose to 9 an over. Graham Strickland went at a gallop, hitting 3 huge sixes in the 35th over, bowled by Makinson, and with 22 scored off his last over Harome were right back in the match. Needham turned to the young Sylvester's off-spin to bowl out the rest of the overs. He did more than that. He bowled out the innings, taking 4 wickets for 17 in his 5 overs. Harome needed 19 off the last over; only two were scored before Greenlay was stumped by Mitchell of Sylvester. The youngster, who had top scored for St Fagan's, then proved the match-winner with the ball.

Happy days, happy times. For every winner, there have been over the years between six hundred and fifty and seven hundred and ninety village cricket clubs who have had to face the disappointment of defeat - their dreams shattered. The one round *not* to lose is the semi-final. Spare a thought then for Langleybury, the most successful of all the Hertfordshire sides. In 1986, they lost their fifth semi-final in a replay at Ynysygerwn. The Langleybury ladies did not know whether to laugh or cry, so managed to do both at the same time. The Welsh felt for them all and a great party took place. Both sides were most gracious and generous in elation and desperation. *The Cricketer*, Ben and Belinda Brocklehurst and all their staff, have not only organised the championship on a day-to-day basis, they have inspired in villages throughout the land the sense of fair play, generosity in defeat, humility in victory, and the playing of the game for the sake of the game. That is a rare commodity in these days of vaulting ambitions centred round financial reward and where the disease of Packeritis can be seen throughout all grades of cricket.

Sources

The Cricketer International Magazine 1971 - 1991
The Village Cricket Handbook 1974 - 1992
The Haig Book of Village Cricket by John Fogg (Pelham Books, 1972).

T.A.L. HUSKINSON